BANGKOK ANGEL

Mike Smith

—————— ✦ ——————

MUSICLINE
PUBLICATIONS

PUBLISHED BY MUSICLINE PUBLICATIONS LTD.

MUSICLINE PUBLICATIONS
Office 5, Mill House, Tolsons Mill, Lichfield Street, Fazeley,
Staffordshire B78, United Kingdom

This edition first published 2000

Printed in Thailand by Allied Printers

Design and typeset by i2i-media

ISBN 1 898754 23 3

BANGKOK ANGEL

Over fifty per-cent of marriages in the UK end in divorce! Dating/marriage agencies have never had it so good. Many middle aged lonely divorced people turn to such agencies in desperation to kick start their lives. One such lonely, downtrodden, divorced man was Mike. At forty eight and living with two children, two cats, two chinchillas, one dog and a cocateil with perfect pitch he felt the need to look for a new partner before all his hair and teeth fell out. So armed with a bottle of light oak hair colour, and aftershave that was guaranteed to be alluring, he began a journey that would eventually take him to the other side of the world in his search for a new wife.

Bangkok Angel is the humorous racy story of that journey to Thailand, told with a refreshing 'my life an open book' honesty.

It will make you laugh. It will make you cry. It may well help you make a decision!

1. Fagin's Den

Beads of sweat rolled down my neck and nestled in the limp lettuce of my spinal column. I had most certainly arrived. How the hell do people live here!

It was four-thirty in the morning Thai time and the airport of the hottest city in the world was still asleep staffed by four officials in passport control who took sadistic pleasure in giving a decent allocation of their working day to each arriving passenger. Air travel may be the fastest mode of transport but none of the travel brochures told me of the ensuing hassle encountered by every weary traveller. It took over an hour to get through this and by the time I was collecting my luggage I was sweating heavily and had lost about four pounds in weight. I melted, relieved into a taxi with air conditioning and revived myself sufficiently to take in the assault of sights. Anyone who thought that London had traffic problems had not experienced Bangkok. At six in the morning it was a chaotic parking lot of sweating humanity. The whole population it seemed was on it's way to work, crammed, like raw prawns into buses without windows. Young girls rode side saddle, perched precariously on the backs of motor bikes and Tuk Tuks, little three wheelers probably invented by someone with a sense of humour, careered, twisted and jammed themselves into every square inch of roasting tarmac.

Legislation as to the condition of vehicles was obviously non-existent and condemned wrecks with world weary springs rattled and banged in a cacophonic symphony while emitting every toxic substance injurious to health into the suffocating pollution of the streets. Whoever had the responsibility for checking exhaust emissions was not very good at his job and was probably the same person who was selling the white face masks to the traffic police who conducted a concerto of manic complexity with little white batons. Everywhere one looked there were stick insect cranes hovering over half built skyscrapers and my first overall impression of Bangkok was that it would look great when someone got around to finishing it.

Eventually I arrived at my small hotel, just off the Sukhumvit Road. From behind a seemingly deserted highly polished reception desk rose a big smile followed by a little face. The girl greeted me in perfect English.

'Good morning sir. Welcome to Bangkok. I trust you had a good trip?'

'Thank you. I had a very good trip,' I lied. 'Is it always this hot and sticky in Bangkok?' I inquired, mopping my face with a soggy white handkerchief.

'It get much hotter than now, sir. This is cool season.' she replied.

Her smile, accompanying this piece of really good news, echoed the beautiful Thai air stewardess I had encountered on the plane, and inspired in me a readiness to trust. In the next few days I would learn more about this gem, called Jym.

She showed me to my room. I could ask no more. It was spotless and had an air conditioner. I fell in love with the air conditioner. From my window on the fourth floor I had a very good view over part of the city. There were lots of modern high rise buildings, mostly hotels I think. In the near distance The Landmark lived up to it's name rising high above the rest. In a small garden, directly below me, a man dressed in only a towel was sitting on a wooden stool washing his feet in a metal bowl.

As I unpacked I realised that most of the clothes I had brought with me were unwearable in this climate, and so a good half of them stayed in the suitcase. Then luxuriating in the shower I cast my mind back to the last conversation I'd had with my very good friend Wilf back home in England.

'Yer ravin' mad pal!'

'Thanks a lot Wilf.'

'No, seriously Mick, what's so wrong with British women?'

'Well besides the fact that they're never bloody satisfied, always trying to change you, and all trying to be men, they're fine Wilf.'

'Okay yes, granted you've had a few bad experiences Mick, but one cuckoo doesn't make a swallow.'

'I think you mean one swallow doesn't make a summer Wilf.'

'Whatever, Mick, whatever.'

'I've got to do something with my life, Wilf, you said so yourself. I don't like being on my own, I need someone to share my life. As I've now got the freedom and opportunity to go and have a look, why not?'

'Okay pal, take your point, but Bangkok!'

'What's so wrong with Bangkok?'

'Well you hear such terrible stories, Mick. Sex and drugs, drugs and sex. I was only reading an article the other day in The Sun.....'

'Look Wilf, I'm sorry we can't agree on this but I've made my decision, bought my air ticket, and tomorrow I'm going, no matter what it says in The Sun!'

'*Sad Git Seeks Meaningful Lay*' is what it's going to say in The Sun, Mick.'

'You are so basic at times, Wilf! I really wish you could understand.'

'Ravin' mad pal! It'll all end in tears.'

'Thank you Wilf!'

'My pleasure Mick!'

England now seemed on another planet and my destiny lay in meeting Lisa, the lady at the top of my list, chosen from a video containing over five hundred Thai ladies who were all, apparently, looking for western husbands. I had written to her and she had replied enclosing a small photograph of herself. She looked very beautiful, but would she be the lady of my dreams? In truth I had just traveled to the other side of the world on the strength of a few fractured lines from a girl I'd never met. Examined logically, as my friends had done, this was insanity. This was craziness piled on top of insanity. Would all this end in disaster? Was I really a sad git as Wilf had intimated? Only time would tell and as it was now nearing the appointed time to telephone the agency I dried myself, dressed, and gave my revived body an overdose of passion lotion. I then dialled the agency number. A man answered whose voice I recognised straight away. It was the same boring, droning voice I had heard five hundred times on the video back in England.

'Welcome to Bangkok Mr. Smith. If you wait at your hotel I will send someone over immediately to escort you to my offices.' I went down to reception and waited. Shortly a large colourful umbrella arrived attached to a young lady who requested me to follow her. The offices were fortunately only a short walk away, but even so the sweat was pouring from the whole of my body again. Some bloody cool season this was! The umbrella turned from the main street and proceeded up a dusty track where insects buzzed like miniature helicopters. The umbrella then halted at a weary looking tin-roofed shack, lowered itself and disappeared within. I followed sceptically. I had imagined that the agency would resemble a sort of travel agent's edifice, smart and cool. Not so! As my eyes adjusted to the contrasting darkness I slowly took in the seediness of my surroundings. It was dark, dirty and dingy. The curtains had been new when the shack was new but they had died on the gallows of neglect. The middle aged man who offered his hand in greeting wore clothes that closely resembled the curtains. His smile was practised and an icicle formed in the air.

'Good to see you Mr. Smith, I trust you had a good flight and that the hotel is to your satisfaction?' the voice from the video hissed, and without waiting for confirmation continued, 'May I suggest we go first to the bank for the agency's fee.'

My first instinct was to run, to get away from this seedy looking, obnoxious little man. I was looking into the face of Fagin. With every look, every move and mannerism he oozed it. I had seen his double on stage many times but this anaemic looking creep was not dealing in little boys, he was dealing in little Thai ladies. Fagin he was and Fagin he remained. Why I didn't flee as my instinct told me remains a mystery. Perhaps it was that also in the office were several other western men, all respectable and smart, and an unmistakable sing song Welsh voice that I readily recognised. The English branch of the Thai marriage agency had put me in contact with a man called Clive. He had already been to Bangkok, met a lady called Karla, and got engaged. His enthusiasm on the telephone had encouraged me to make this trip. He assured me that he had found great happiness, and that there were many beautiful Thai ladies all looking for western husbands. His voice now had form. We introduced ourselves. He wasn't quite what I expected. He was a lot taller than I had pictured him in my mind but the voice was the same, and in the circumstances that in itself was reassuring. He introduced me to Karla who was lovely, very shy and innocent looking. She spoke only a few words of English so conversation was limited. Clive had only just started to tell me about his forthcoming Buddhist wedding in the north of Thailand when Fagin quickly intervened with an air of impatience.

'Mr. Smith, if you are now ready we really should make our way to the bank to take advantage of the extremely gratifying exchange rate of thirty eight point six. There are, I assure you, many beautiful ladies who would like to meet you. It will only take a moment if you please.'

Fagin slimed from his office and led me across the street to the bank where I handed over the five hundred pound fee. It hurt! We then returned to the shack.

'Lisa, your number one choice, will be arriving shortly Mr. Smith. In the meantime perhaps you would care to meet some of our other available ladies. We take very great care to ensure that all our ladies are respectable and would ask that you conduct yourself accordingly.'

'Conduct myself how?' I asked with a fair degree of annoyance. What did he think I was going to do, jump on them? This muppet man was really getting up my nose.

Fagin ignored my reply and with a wave of his arm ushered me up some stairs and into a private sitting room that had the same crumpled look as the main office. Furnished with a plastic wood effect coffee table and four tired armchairs, it reminded me of many school staff-rooms I had once known well. A girl entered. She was gorgeous, tall, slim like a model and spoke very good English. She was well educated, attending university, but only seventeen years old. I was utterly dumbfounded. We talked for a while and she gave me every indication that she would like to see me again. No way could this girl be interested in me, not for the right reasons anyway. I searched hurriedly for an escape. It was short and unrehearsed, 'I have many other ladies to meet and I'll be in touch. Thank-you very much for coming to meet me.'

This was weird. She was everything a hot-bloodied male could possibly want and I sent her away. Two more girls were brought in to meet me, both a little older but still far too young. This was not what I had travelled seven thousand miles to see. This was not what I wanted or expected. Of course I wished to meet an attractive lady but she would have to be a little more mature than these. I might well be lonely and desperate but what did Fagin think I was, a middle-aged pervert! The whole exercise was too clinical, too artificial. It felt as if I was there to purchase a woman. The goods were paraded and I could pick and choose at will. This was an unreal situation in a world I did not comprehend. There was definitely something missing, and where the hell was Lisa?

Fagin entered the room. His face was pale as though it never saw the sun and his legs hung like plucked chickens from beneath a pair of shorts so patched and darned that little of the original remained. Uriah like, his voice droned a familiar pattern.

'Have you met someone you like the look of, Mr. Smith?' fingered Fagin.

'I like them all, they're lovely girls, who wouldn't like them? But they are all far too young. I'm looking for a saloon, not a sports car!' I replied in a light hearted jovial sort of way, seeking not to offend.

'Age doesn't matter here Mr. Smith, they are all looking for security.' Fagin responded with a definite air of superiority. As he didn't seem to have a sense of humour, and obviously hadn't understood, I tried again a little more forcibly.

'That may well be true, but you've obviously never met my mother and England is not Thailand. I'm forty eight years old. Don't you think I'd look a bit stupid walking down my local high street with a girl on my arm only two years older than my daughter? What I'm looking for here is a lady to share my life, not an immature schoolgirl to share my bed! I thought I had made this clear to you in my original correspondence.'

Fagin's throat made a noise that seemed to indicate it was trying to push something into his mouth, and his superiority collapsed like a pack of playing cards.

'I take your point Mr. Smith, I take your point. Please be assured that Lisa will be here very soon. As you know she is twenty nine and I am certain will be more to your liking.'

At about five o'clock Lisa arrived. Fagin faded into the curtains.

She was just as lovely as she had appeared in the video. Something stirred. She was slightly smaller than me, and her hair hung black and long. The jeans she was wearing had been sprayed on with loving care to more than adequately compliment her slim feminine form. Her smile was warm and encouraging. Unfortunately she spoke no English at all, so one of the office girls had to translate for us. I had been told originally that her English was fair but all she seemed to know was the way to McDonald's. That's as good a starting place as any I thought as my optimism gathered pace. Why let language be a problem, she's very attractive. I can learn Thai and she can learn English. Together we bought a dictionary each and with interpreter in tow we headed for the burger house.

Thus, getting to know you, had made a start and concluded with a promise to meet the next day to do a Temple. I now felt more encouraged and examined my discoveries on the way back to the hotel. Lisa worked in a large department store selling jeans and had been married to a Thai who had met an untimely end in a motorcycle accident. This fact, though sad, didn't surprise me as all the young men I had seen on motorbikes so far in Bangkok seemed to have a death wish. She was nearly thirty and a Buddhist, not surprising in a land of over ninety per cent Buddhists. And she knew McDonald's

My steam gave out. I was very tired. It had been a long day. Coffee at Heathrow, to take away Thai burger, had been some leap. Satisfied with everything except the plucked chicken in shorts, I approached the entrance to my hotel and planned to have a shower, relax with a book and fall to sleep, perchance to dream.

Somewhere Buddha smiled without moving his lips.

Inside the hotel Clive was sitting in reception with a friend who he introduced as Martin. He had met Martin on his first trip to Bangkok and had asked him to be best man at his wedding in a few days time. I very much warmed to Martin right away. He had a good sense of fun and didn't seem to take life too seriously. Clive, perhaps preoccupied with his forthcoming nuptials, excused himself to go for a walk and left his best man to the tender mercies of this green, inquisitive Englishman. Martin had been to Thailand several times before and had also worked in the Middle and Far East so his experience was invaluable. I had a thousand questions and eagerly lapped up the information and advice Martin was able, and willing, to give. He enthused as he warmed to his theme though in no time at all he succumbed to grief and was pouring out his heartfelt woes. In short, my new friend had met via the agency, a Thai beautician called Ning Nong, and had fallen madly in love. She was, however, giving him grief on a stick. He was confused and in anguish. He didn't know where he stood with her, mainly because she was a master at the art of evading confrontation. In the good old days when Thailand was Siam, the bringer of bad news always had his head cut off - a quaint old custom that must still linger in the Thai subconscious. Unlike Clive, who had, so to speak, scored, Martin had not even been awarded a penalty. What started out as a fact finding chat ended with myself in the uneasy role of father confessor as this new met friend poured out his pain in a way one can do so readily with a total stranger. I sympathised with him, listened a lot and gave him the benefit of my vast experience of Thai women, culminating with a critical appraisal of McDonald's I

I must have had some effect because by the time I'd finished he looked close to tears. I tried humour,

'It's hell of a name for a girl Martin, '*Do you Martin take thee Ning Nong*' may well cause a degree of hilarity in an English church.'

It didn't work. He seemed utterly determined to drown in his pint of lager. Having utterly failed as a counsellor I decided to leave him to wallow in his pool of pity, and get some sleep. I made my excuses, said goodnight to Jym as I passed by reception, and retreated to my bed.

Buddha's smile teetered on a chuckle, and somewhere in the middle distance a band in a bar played a bum note. I slept. Bangkok didn't.

2. Intrigue and Deception

The following day we met early in the morning to 'do a Temple.' The stairway leading to the upper terraces were, even at this early hour, milling with tourists. I didn't feel so much like a tourist, more a man on a mission and all else was secondary to my primary purpose. Nevertheless, when in Bangkok -

Phra Pai, God of the Wind, stared into the lens of my camera as Lisa and I clicked our way up the artificial mountain of Wat Arun, The Temple of Dawn. Like a stepped pyramid, Mount Meru stretched to its topmost heaven guarded by a ring of demons in stone. Four great staircases, any one of which could be ascended, was reached through a pavilion housing an image of Buddha, each prang representing a key event in his life. Here in meditation, guarded by a seven headed serpent. From the terrace, across the great Chao Prya river, there was a stunning view of the city bubbling like a cauldron of humanity, and noises of today that argued with the ancient temple mountains reaching higher towards the sun and understanding, and decorated with great blooms of flowers made from broken Chinese pottery. My eyes looked upwards to the pinnacle. Demons, no doubt familiar in stories to every Thai child, guarded the whole edifice and tourists clickety clicked in artificial poses their proof of having been there. This sweltering jewel of the East cooled its toes in the river and canals, the very arteries of the city. Lisa bowed a deep and graceful Wai before Buddha and signed for me to follow suit which I did as a sign of acceptance and courtesy for the girl's beliefs. I was definitely getting my five bahts worth of education here!

For a passing moment I felt the ghosts and ancestors reaching up through the stones. I felt the gaze of the unseeing eyes penetrating my inner thoughts and pondered the complexities of life, the strangeness of it's people, and the mystifying presence stretching across the void of ages. Quietened into such thoughtful contemplation brought me face to face with my own little dilemma, and I felt like a grain of sand in a desert. Voices from the past.

I now knew far more about Buddha than I did about Lisa. I had bought a guide book on Wat Arun, but there was no guide book available on Lisa!

The dictionaries were fairly quickly tossed aside as an impractical method of communication and replaced with sign language and smiles. Lisa's smile was still as inviting and mysterious, but smiles could be misinterpreted. To my western perceptions they gave an indication of approval or acceptance but somehow conveyed an incomplete message. What did a smile mean? Having worked in the past for a Japanese company I had experience of the nod that doesn't mean yes, the shake of the head that doesn't mean no, and the Japanese smile that only rarely means maybe. Thailand and Japan, both far eastern countries, but probably very different. This was more difficult than I had supposed in my first flush of enthusiastic anticipation. I had no way of knowing if she liked me, disliked me, or was just enjoying her ice cream. What was going on behind the face? I still found her attractive, I had no doubts on that score, but somewhere there was a piece missing. Perhaps it was a cultural thing. I still had so much to learn.

The following day we 'did the river.'

The backside of Bangkok was fascinating. It is extraordinary how the best and most informative view of many cities, London, New York, Amsterdam, Paris, is seen from the water. Thus it was with Bangkok. Here on the Chao Phrya and the network of canals, a kaleidoscope of sights assaulted my senses. People here spent their life on the water just as in Hong Kong or Singapore. Everywhere I looked there were traders and merchants. It was as if the Sukhumvit Road had taken to the water. Produce and flowers from up-country were loaded and unloaded at the markets. Tug boats strung great barges together with hawsers and barely crested the waterline. They ploughed against the current while ferry boats ran dangerously at right angles to the traffic. Kitchens too travelled the water as vendors cooked noodles, rice and popcorn and hooted their approach to prospective customers. Lisa and I sat in the rue duan, an express bus of the river, lean long and white with red stripes. A tug chugged by proudly displaying sharks teeth on the prow, her long tail throwing up spray at the sampans and bum boats.

I soon realised that the art of travelling by water in Bangkok was permanently to carry around a large cushion as the vibration of the noisy engines travelled through the wooden seats to a tender part of my anatomy. I gazed in fascination at the children fishing, diving and splashing and the old men casting nets to catch silvery fish and people everywhere sloshing out their watery lives. I reflected that, as a kid, I too would have joined in the cooling pleasures of the river and tightrope walked the hawsers connecting the barges, and ignore the dangers as these kids did.

I looked through the lens of my camera across the panorama of the rooftops, at Wat Arun where yesterday we had climbed, and along the fading elegant houses and mansions from another age and to the Grand Palace. It's roof throwing back the sunlight in exotic radiance. There was so much to take in. On the far bank I could see what must be the royal barges, long elegant and ornate. By the water's edge a diver surfaced amidst bubbles and grasped what seemed to be old junk from the river bed, the detritus of the city.

Lisa sat and bounced in unison with the engine and looked upon her city as if from new eyes and smiled and pointed this way and that. Her outstretched hand conveyed to me the sights, her smile conveyed nothing. My thousand questions remained unanswered.

On the Thonburi side of the river were the klongs, canals that enter into a world of thickening jungle and coconut plantations. Perched on the banks were houses on stilts top heavy with families cooking and eating. The children squealed and bathed the banks in innocent delight. Through the tangle of lush undergrowth I spied yet another temple to Buddha made mysterious by the foliage of the dancing trees and long lush grasses. The palm trees overhung the canal in an archway that created shadows and shafts of light alternately. It was a journey into old Thailand, how it used to be before the west arrived. Tropical birds hung in the branches, great splashes of colour reflecting the sunlight like stained glass windows in a cathedral of greenery. The mind however, could only take in as much as the bum could endure and for this alone I welcomed the chugging end to our journey.

As a deaf and dumb tour guide Lisa was excellent. I was enjoying the trips but slowly forming the impression that often she didn't seem to have a clue what was happening. Our inability to communicate with language was now a very real problem. I arranged to meet her at the agency office so that we could use the interpreter again.

In Fagin's office the shadows lurked. It took quite a while to accustom my eyes to the contrasting dimness after the glaring brightness of outside in the dusty street. Fagin's legs clucked into view from the shadows, closely followed by the shorts and shirt that seemed to grow out of his pores. He hadn't changed. His face then slithered into sight. We all sat down and I asked him to asses for me how Lisa was feeling. Did she wish to carry on seeing me or would she prefer to call it a day? Fagin spoke about ten words to her in Thai. Lisa replied, smiling broadly, with about half as many words. Fagin then turned to me and said,
'She will marry you Mr. Smith.'

Suddenly I had a headache, a really bad headache and my feet wanted to run. What the hell was this man doing. I needed distance and time to think. Things were happening far too fast for me and I couldn't keep pace. Running from the clutches of Fagin could well become habit forming! I had no wish to be rude to Lisa, it wasn't her fault, she was as much a pawn in this game as I was. My mind searched again for an escape, and was again unrehearsed. I thanked Lisa for saying that she would like to marry me and suggested we go for a meal later with the interpreter to discuss the matter further. They both looked puzzled. I further excused myself with the ploy of an expected phone call from England. Fagin spoke to Lisa who nodded her approval to meet again later.

With that agreed I quickly escaped, leaving them both at the agency, retraced my steps along the now familiar dirt track, and returned to my hotel. Instinct told me that this was not how things were meant to be. I was on a roller coaster ride and couldn't get off. Where was Martin ? Where was Clive? I needed the safety net of their company but unfortunately they had already departed up north for Clive's wedding. I sat down in reception, ordered a coffee, and pondered my dilemma. I knew I needed to take charge of events and not be subject to them as I now was. I slowly disentangled myself from the roller coaster in my head and started to get a grip on reality again. Fagin had really dropped me in it here. Or was this how it normally happened? I just didn't know. I had no idea if I wanted to marry this girl. I didn't even know her well enough to hold her hand. I was so obviously being manipulated, and it was going to have to stop. I could hear my father's voice saying, 'It's all a lot of silliness Michael.' And that's about the truth, Dad!

I stiffened my sinews, decided to go for the meal and try to back-pedal the situation. But how?

We met at the agency at eight, myself, Lisa, and surprisingly Fagin's wife. She was Thai but unusually tall, attractive in an odd sort of way but I perceived there was little eye contact when she talked. Although she spoke very good English I felt the same unease and distrust I had felt from the start with her husband. My life in their hands. Oh dear!

The pub chosen for the meeting was called 'Cabbages and Condoms.' A quaint name for a pub, acquired because it was built on ground that used to be the garden plot of the birth control centre. Each wooden table was fringed with manicured bushes that provided privacy except for the emaciated Siamese cats that prowled for scraps of food. We all sat outside in this delightful pub garden where fairy lights twinkled and danced in the overhanging trees. All in all a very romantic setting. Another time and different company, it would be ideal.

I felt a tension in the air as I groped to take control.

'Do you know Lisa well?' I asked Mrs. Fagin.

'Yes I do,' she replied, turning her gaze on the girl. 'She is a lovely and respectable Thai lady.'

Her words held all the appeal of a sales pitch and the air was punctuated by a gong somewhere in the darkness.

The food was served but held very little interest for me as I picked my way through the cabbages of the conversation. Mrs. Fagin took great pains to impress on me that Lisa thought I was wonderful and that we were engaged. Time for the brakes had arrived!

The fairy lights danced and tinkled a chorus of mocking laughter and waited like smiling spies for the outcome.

'While I find Lisa very attractive,' I stumbled. 'I did not ask your husband to put the question of marriage to her at all and feel we need more time to get to know each other better. All I wanted from your husband was some indication as to Lisa's willingness, or otherwise, to carry on seeing me.'

Mrs. Fagin turned to Lisa and ricocheted a few words at her in Thai. Lisa smiled and nodded like a dog in the back windscreen of a taxi.

'Do you think that Lisa is a bright and intelligent girl? I heard my doubts put into words.

'Oh yes.' replied the sales lady. 'I think she is, though she hasn't had enough education to bring out her full potential.'

The fairy lights responded in tinkling chatter. I desperately looked down at the cats for guidance who returned my smile longingly for the scraps of my heart on a plate.

The poisoned beanpole seemed to sense a serious disquiet

'Why don't you continue to get to know each other better, Mr. Smith? Do not worry. Although you are deemed to be engaged you may change your mind if you so wish.'

Satisfied with this as a solution we all parted company. The cats swarmed for scraps around the vacated table.

The mists of doubt concerning Lisa cleared the next day when we took a trip to the coast. Lisa was accompanied by her younger sister Dara, who was equally as beautiful though she too spoke no English. At least I could now practice my sign language in stereo! There was however a pervading difference between the sisters, and it was all in the eyes. Dara was a bright and intelligent girl. The comparison was obvious now and I could see it very clearly. Lisa did not radiate understanding but the younger sister did, and her whole being showed it.

I had been taking pictures all day, and having come to the end of a film set the camera to rewind. It unfortunately got stuck in the middle, though the realisation came only when I opened the camera. The film was exposed and ruined. With dismay I tore it from the camera to throw away, but Lisa intervened, and taking it from me marched off to a processing booth, ignoring not only my awkward attempts to tell her that this was a waste of time, but also Dara's attempts at the same explanation in Thai. Lisa had no concept. It was sad really and only reinforced what was growingly apparent. I now knew what I had to do, but her motivations still intrigued me.

We eventually returned to my hotel and as usual Lisa waited in reception for me. From my room I spoke on the telephone to Jym in reception. She was well aware of my situation and quickly grasped her role. She would engage Lisa in conversation and try to assess her motives, and her opinion of me. When Jym returned my call the die was cast. She assessed Lisa as nice but fairly dim. She wasn't crazy about me at all but felt that her future life held a choice of two routes, marriage to a western man, or working as a seamstress in a Taiwan factory. I was apparently thought to be a marginally better option. I had no reason to distrust Jym's sincerity as her only purpose was to be of help to a guest. This confirmed all my doubts.

I returned to reception and with Jym's help talked to Lisa. I told her that I could not marry her. I explained that I felt we had both been manipulated by the agency and rushed into making decisions before we were ready. I apologised, and with tears in her eyes she left the hotel. I felt like a heel and pitied her. She wasn't a bad girl, she was just being used. The agency had promised to find her a western husband and a good bride price. This is an amount of money paid to the girl's parents by the future husband, and varies as to the social status of the girl concerned. The agency had got it all sewn up. They would also exact a further fee from me having achieved their primary purpose of finding me a wife. What a mess!

Within an hour Fagin was on the phone asking me what the hell I thought I was doing as he had Lisa sobbing her heart out in his office. I told him that I didn't appreciate being lied to, wanted my money refunded, and thought he should take a lot more care when dealing with people's lives in future. He calmed down immediately and asked me if I would like to meet any more girls. I think, if memory serves me correctly, I used a profound obscenity and put the phone down.

The agency roller coaster had come to an abrupt halt. How could I have been so gullible? To say the least, I felt sick. I had been a fool and all I wanted now was to go home.

The all knowing, all seeing Buddha smiled his broadest smile.

3. The Dating Game

I thought of home, my children, my friends and especially the grief that Wilf would give me was too painful to consider. I'd had it with agencies, England had failed me and now Bangkok had failed me. I looked from the well of my self pity and despaired at the climb. The fascination of my surroundings palled. I couldn't wait to get back on the plane but that was four days away. I lay on my bed and wallowed. The muffled drone of the air conditioner hypnotically transported my mind back through the events that had led me here.

It had taken some time to sweep up the carnage of my first marriage. I had the custody of my two children, Emma and David, and a living to make. There had been little time left to socialise and an essential ingredient of my happiness was missing. My friends were all married or in relationships. I could not see myself pretending to be a young man again and getting out there with the trendies. The only sensible solution it seemed was a dating agency. I thought it would at least allow me to get started in the availability market and would help to re-establish my social skills with the ladies. I had placed an advert in the local paper, 'Getting To Know You' section. I felt like a faded pop group trying a comeback.

Gentleman 48, 5'7", blue eyes, own teeth, two tone coloured hair, seeks lady with good sense of humour to share overdraft facility.
Must like music, children and animals.
(Wild parties and sex orgies optional).

You would have thought that having placed such a deep and meaningful advertisement that I would have received more than one reply. Look on the positive side I thought, she might be a vision of loveliness. Okay, I didn't have that sort of luck selling double glazing, but you never know.

We agreed to meet at nine in the evening outside a local

pub. I must emphasise here that I had gone to a fair bit of trouble 'titivating myself up a bit'. I'd belted down to the chemist to purchase a bottle of light oak hair colour. It was good fun administering it to my head and most of the bathroom surfaces. Luckily the final effect in the mirror was amazing, no grey, and I looked ten years younger. (That's five years plus wishful thinking!) I then ironed my best shirt and trousers, cleaned the car, shaved, and brushed my teeth till they shone. The after-shave I splashed on all over was guaranteed to be seductive and alluring. It said so on the box. So I was ready. Oh boy was I ready!

I arrived early, about ten to nine and waited for her red car to turn off the main road and into the pub car park. Nine o'clock- no red car. Two blue ones, a black one, a grotty old van but no red car. Ten past nine and a sense of intense relief was creeping over me. She wasn't going to turn up. Then, suddenly a red car appeared. 'Oh shit! She's here!' Quick, put out the fag. A quick blast down my throat with the extra strong peppermint spray and I'm ready. Please be gentle with me.

She looked like she'd just walked from Land's End on a protest march. Jeans, no make-up, pumps and the piece de re-sistance, a very sexless, long and grubby, green anorak. Why, I thought, had I gone to all this trouble to look my best? Oh well, you can't necessarily judge a book by its cover. Yes, you bloody well can! The clothes completely and utterly suited this girl. In the pub I bought her a drink and asked her to tell me a little bit about herself. She didn't draw breath till ten to eleven. I think, personally, that she was a Russian women's lib activist but I could have been wrong. I had never met anyone before with whom I had absolutely nothing in common. At eleven fifteen, back in the car park, I made my excuses and left. I think, probably, she was as relieved as I was.

I once read an American book on the psychology of selling. One paragraph of that book came to mind following this first failed encounter into the wild, wild, wood.

'You knock on one hundred doors. You are successful in

making ten appointments. You manage to get into three houses and make your sales pitch. You make one sale from which you earn £100 commission. Don't say how great it is to make £100 in one hour. Say rather, every time a door is slammed in your face, thanks very much for the pound!'

So with this excellent philosophy in mind, 'thank you very much for the pound', I decided to move onward to the next door. I still had to find the door though. The deep and meaningful advertisement yielded no more response, so I joined a proper dating agency. By 'proper' I mean a company that collects addresses of lonely people, puts them in a pamphlet and sells them to other lonely people. Being one such lonely person myself at the time, it did serve a purpose. It found me the doors to knock on. So I telephoned several ladies and several ladies telephoned me.

One conversation, that didn't actually lead to a date, was interesting. She was an Irish girl with a lovely Gaelic lilt to her voice but she was utterly obsessed with the exploits of her previous lover. She kept saying, 'Do you know what he did then?' Following which she recounted the dreadful things that had been done to her both emotionally and physically. All I could do was to sympathise and assure her that she was probably better off without him as he sounded a bit of a prat but she kept on and on, one story after another. I felt really sorry for her and didn't have the heart to put the phone down despite it being all a bit heavy and very personal. Then she said,
'How would you feel if I asked you to dress up as a cowboy?'
I put the phone down.

The next actual date I went on, following one of these intense and delving telephone conversations, was slightly more fruitful. It resulted in a relationship that lasted about two weeks. I turned up at her house at the appointed time having made the same supreme effort to look reasonable as before, and with the same 'knock their suspenders off' after-shave oozing from every available bit of bare flesh. The door opened. 'Oh bliss! Oh joy!' She looked great and obviously had gone to the same amount of trouble to make herself presentable as I had. She was blonde, about my height, fairly slim and with what can only be described as a more than adequate cleavage bulging out of a delightfully low cut black evening dress. She invited me in and kindly offered me a cup of coffee. Naturally, I accepted. While the kettle was coming to the boil we chatted, she, leaning on one side of the breakfast bar and me, facing her, leaning on the other side. I was having great trouble averting my eyes from that magnificent bulging cleavage. She smiled and I heard myself say,

'You are a very attractive lady.'

She could see I was embarrassed and said, still smiling,

'Thirty-eight B cup.'

'Not thirty-eight B cup!' I said with some relief. 'I haven't encountered a thirty-eight B cup since the sixties!'

All tension floated away and we had a great evening getting to know one another. We saw each other three or four times over the following two weeks and then she telephoned me to say she was going to live in Australia with a sheep-shearer who she had been seeing on the nights when she didn't see me. And I thought she was at home knitting! I mean, for goodness sake- a sheep-shearer! Beaten by an Australian sheep-shearer! That's the pits! I wonder what after-shave he used! Beaten and bruised, I returned to the drawing board and threw away the seductive and alluring passion potion. 'Look on the bright side,' I reassured myself. 'Only another ninety eight doors to go!'

Over the following months I met several ladies but no-one who resulted in a second date. It wasn't so much that I was too choosy, there just wasn't anyone I met I would have considered asking my children to live with. It had to be someone special. I had the full support of both my children in this quest. They wanted their dear old Dad to be happy and not lonely but were both well aware that any decision I made was going to considerably affect their lives as well. As I said, it had to be someone very special. As the dates came and went I was beginning to think that I would never be successful.

There was a lady solicitor whose boyfriend phoned me the day after our date and suggested that if I saw her again I was dead. I mean, seriously, how can someone advertise their availability, go out on a date and forget to tell her boyfriend that their relationship is over? She, of course, apologised and assured me it would be all right because although he was a gym instructor and had a black belt in something or other he was very busy at the moment and almost certainly wouldn't have the time to pop over and sort me out. Highly reassuring, I thought. It was nearly a week before I returned my son's cricket bat to the garden shed.

There was a lady teacher who talked all night about - yes, you guessed it - teaching. You can imagine how enormously impressed I was with her. During the time I was teaching, I had developed the habit of telling anyone I should meet on trains, boats and planes that, for a living, I was a roof-felter. Having had many long and tedious chats about the horrendous problems of other people's kids, I adopted the roof-felter pose. I spoke to a doctor once who used to do something similar. He used to say he dealt in animal waste products. Both tactics were designed to kill conversation so that one could get some sleep on a long journey.

Funnily enough the one relationship I did have that lasted a few months didn't come via the agency but from a professional engagement. Musically I used to direct a pantomime for a local theatre group. The pantomime this particular year was Aladdin, and Aladdin was rather nice. It was the first time I had been out with a fella in tights! She was divorced and had two boys both slightly older than my children. We all got on very well and for a couple of months the relationship blossomed. She was an excellent singer and we had much in common but fate was about to test seriously my sense of humour again. She had to come off the pill because her doctor thought it sensible at her age. We had a long discussion about this, both democratically putting forward our opinions. Then she decided that I should do the honourable thing and have a vasectomy. As we had both produced our quota of children it did at the time seem to be the logical thing to do.

The first step was to have a chat with my good friend Wilf who had received the chop two years previously.

'It's a doddle Mick,' he said. 'Nothing to it. Didn't hurt a bit. Onto the table, snip, snip, a cup of tea and out.'

Reassured by this I went to see the doctor and arranged to have the operation done in two weeks time on a Friday afternoon. So, in due course, there I was lying on the table having a chat to the doctor about music while he snipped away. As he snipped the left testicle we chatted about Shostakovich and as he snipped the right testicle we chatted about Schoenberg. Well let me tell you, the guy must not have been too keen on Shostakovich. Six hours later, whilst watching Coronation Street, I passed out with pain. Everything below my waist turned black and increased considerably in size, and I mean everything. I had a willy any black man would have been proud of. I spent two days in greater discomfort than I had ever known, swallowing pain killers on the hour every hour, and doing a great impression of a pregnant duck when I walked. On returning to the doctor on Monday, he took one look at me as I dropped my trousers and said, 'Oh you poor man.' He then left the room to get his camera. Fame at last, I was going to have my picture in The Lancet.

I was not fully operational with the damaged testicles for about six months. Two months after the operation the doctor asked me if I was having any particular sensation on ejaculation. 'Yes,' I said. 'Why? Don't you?' It was the first time I'd ever seen the man smile. Even now, two years later, he apologises to me every time we meet.

My inability to perform up to the required standard and, to be honest, one or two other factors, killed off the relationship. I was back to masturbation as an art form to be able to report back to the doctor how the old sperm count was decreasing. Life really is a bit of a bastard at times! But was I downhearted? You bet your bloody life I was. Was there someone up there who didn't like me? Shouldn't it be someone else's turn for a change? It felt as though someone was punishing me for the misdeeds of my youth and as there had been a fair few of those, how long would this go on for? Let's face it, I'd been divorced, made redundant, been rejected several times and had my tackle hacked to pieces. What else could happen? The one thing that stopped me doing myself in at this stage, was that if something really good had happened the day after, I'd have felt really pissed off!

Around this time I saw an advertisement in a newspaper. I think it was The Guardian. It offered a chance to write to single ladies in Thailand who were looking for western husbands. I telephoned the number given and asked for further details to be sent. A few days later an extremely well produced colour brochure arrived with some photographs of Thai ladies included. Many of them were stunningly attractive but most looked very young. The literature suggested that I should purchase a video which would contain hundreds of available Thai girls. Further, I should watch this carefully and choose seven or eight girls to write to initially. If, after some correspondence, both parties were interested in meeting each other, a trip to Thailand would be necessary.

It all sounded plausible enough, just another dating agency but how much, I thought, would all this cost?

I telephoned the number again and had a long conversation with a gentleman who sounded highly believable, seemed very knowledgeable on this subject and was himself married to a Thai. Now this gentleman was very convincing and sounded utterly sincere, but he was telling me all the things I wanted to hear in my somewhat vulnerable state of mind. If I had done what I should have done at this time I would probably never have gone to Thailand. I should have looked very carefully into this. I should have done some investigating and checked things out but I didn't. I was just excited at the prospect of numerous young and attractive Thai ladies, all apparently willing to get to know me. So I went into this utterly green and with the unenviable ability to hear only what I wanted to hear.

4. The Road to Bangkok

I was hooked, well and truly hooked. I couldn't send my money fast enough. A few days later a package containing the video arrived. The children were at school so I was on my own. I sat down with a cup of tea and stared at the television screen in eager anticipation. One by one the girls paraded in front of my eyes. The video was of very poor quality and my first overall impression was that most of them seemed to have bad teeth. The vocal description of each girl was very short and gave little information.

'This is Miss .... five foot four inches tall - elementary education-works as a dressmaker...'
'This is Miss .... five foot five inches tall - secondary education-works as a food vendor...'

The monotone voice deadened the senses after a while even though many of the girls on offer were incredibly attractive. Endless cups of tea and a full ashtray later, saw the completion of my task. I had looked at about five-hundred girls. Their ages ranged from nineteen to thirty-eight, and most were under five feet six inches tall. I remember regretting not having discovered this country much earlier in my life, which would have saved me nearly crippling myself from the folded handkerchiefs stuffed into the heels of my shoes!

All I had to do now was to choose eight of them to write to. Not a simple task at all. It was easy to choose one but eight was going to be difficult. There was one particular girl who caught my eye. She was very attractive, slim, twenty-eight years old, worked in a department store and had secondary education. Her name was Lisa and she went to the top of my list. The other seven were chosen with difficulty and I sent my completed list back to the agency with a short letter for each of the girls containing a photograph of myself.

I found out from my local post office that it takes about five days for a letter to reach Thailand and vice-versa. So after ten days exactly, I phoned the agency to see if there were any replies. There was one, from the girl at the top of my list. The man at the agency said he thought she must be very interested in me as she had replied so quickly.

The letter that eventually arrived was short but very encouraging. She said she thought I was handsome and charming. Now this was more like it, I thought. She said she was very eager to meet me and asked if it was possible for me to visit Bangkok soon? The photograph she had included with the letter showed her to be even more attractive than on the video. I was not only well hooked now but ready to be reeled in. Very quickly I was back on the phone to the agency to discuss the various routes to Thailand. I've always been a bit on the impulsive side but this was me at my worst. I felt ten years younger. There was a spring in my step. There was a smile on my face and my backache had suddenly disappeared. I kept looking at Lisa's photograph and dreamed of meeting her for the first time. I knew that she did not speak very much English but that didn't matter. I could teach her. Every negative thought was now, very successfully, being turned into a positive thought.

It was suggested by the agency that I fly Thai Airways as this was my first trip. They said it was a direct flight from London Heathrow to Bangkok and that I would get a flavour of Thailand the moment I got onto the plane. The air hostesses would all be Thai and halfway to Bangkok they would change into traditional Thai costume and serve Thai food. This sounded good to me and infinitely preferable to going up the chippie, but obviously a lot more expensive. From several talks I had with the agency it became clear that this was going to cost a considerable amount of money. There was the English agency fee payable before I left, the Thai agency fee payable on arrival in Bangkok, the return air fare, accommodation and spending money. I was probably looking at a total figure of around two thousand pounds for the two week trip. It would, therefore, take the majority of my savings to do this thing. I convinced myself that I could always work harder when I got back to boost the funds. Another negative successfully kicked into touch!

It was interesting, right from the start, to observe the reaction of my friends and family to the direction my life was going. I learned a lot about all of them during this period. This story isn't just about me, as will become apparent. It's about many people and the primary purpose of their actions.

The agency, keen to ensure my eagerness to go to Thailand, put me in touch with a man called Clive who had already visited Bangkok earlier in the year, met a Thai lady called Karla and had got engaged. Our first telephone conversation put the icing on the cake in relation to my decision to go to Thailand. Clive was utterly reassuring about the agency and confirmed that there were many genuine and beautiful Thai ladies out there eager to meet single western men. He was returning to Thailand in October to marry Karla. We had several conversations which in the end persuaded me to go to Bangkok at the same time as Clive, and stay at the same hotel. This seemed sensible because then at least I would not be utterly on my own and Clive knew a lot more than I about the country. Although he was about ten years younger than I, we had a fair bit in common with each other. He was also divorced and had a son and daughter the same ages as my children. Clive waxed lyrical about Thailand and Karla. Here was a man utterly convinced that he had met his dream lady. Being Welsh, he was a prolific conversationalist and none of our telephone chats, during the next year, were short. We cost each other a fortune boosting the profits of British Telecom.

The decision was made to go. The required amount of money was paid to the agency. The air tickets and hotel were booked. All I had to do was wait until October. During this six week period I had another three letters from other girls on my list. They all looked lovely but all said very similar things in their letters and all wanted me to go to Bangkok as quickly as I could to meet them. It occurred to me that the agency in Bangkok most certainly helped these girls to write their letters. In my naivetâ I thought this was probably because the girls' knowledge of the English language was limited.

I had many things to arrange before I skipped off to the other side of the world. My children, and Oscar the dog, would have to go and stay with my ex-wife. My business partner, Keith, would have to be sweet-talked into holding the fort alone while I was away. Someone would have to feed Fluffy and Sheba, the cats and my mother would have to be told where I was going.

My ex-wife was willing to have the children and the dog. Keith was very supportive because, above all, he thought I needed a holiday and my next door neighbour, Janet, agreed to feed the cats. This left only one bridge to cross and was always going to be the tricky one. I couldn't tell my mother the complete truth as she would have threatened to leave all her money to the dogs' home again. I feared that she would not be at all understanding or supportive.

My mother is a force to be reckoned with, never wrong and an opinion about everything. Five foot one with a six foot tongue and still going strong at eighty-six. She fought family and neighbours - and won. She fought the Midland Bus Company - and won. If Hitler had invaded, she would, single-handedly, have posed a serious danger to shipping! She still fights with me, her one and only loving son.

A good education was an obsession with my mother, instilled into her by her mother who was unable to afford good schooling for her own children. As there was not a state school 'good enough' in the area, my parents went without many things to send me to a private junior school. I was lucky and passed the eleven-plus to get into the local Grammar School. Academically I did not make the most of my time there. Sport and girls were of much more interest than studying. Inevitably I failed most of my exams and was forced to spend a humiliating time repeating my fifth year while all my friends exuded 'street cred' in the sixth form. The worst part of this was still having to wear the less than flattering school cap which was utterly degrading. I did, however, learn a valuable lesson. You tend to get in life what you deserve, except for the dreaded school cap! No one deserves to have to wear one no matter how bad they are.

I decided to tell her that I was going to Bangkok because I needed a holiday. Straight away she said that if I got involved with one of those Asian girls she would leave all her money to the dogs' home. I always knew she would be a bridge too far! She's a great lady, on the whole. Great to have on your side when you're doing what she approves of but if I had only ever done what my mother approved of, I would still be in teaching and a right boring old fart! My father I think would have been more understanding.

At the age of six, he shoved a very large violin under my very small chin. Dad was an amateur musician and a painter of some quality. Above all he was a gentleman. He would offer his seat to a lady on a crowded bus; remove his hat as a funeral cortege passed by and would sum up the troubles of mankind, including the first and second world wars as 'a lot of silliness'. He idolised Kathleen Ferrier, Yehudi Menuhin and an oboist whose name escapes me. He worked at a steel factory in the midlands for over forty years during which time he only ever had one day off, when he broke his collarbone. When he finally retired he actually didn't, he wasn't the type to potter about. He became a peripatetic instrumental teacher which gave him enormous pleasure and satisfaction. On telling stories of his youth there would be a smile on his face as he recounted tales of music played and pictures painted until his expression changed as he uttered the final comment, 'And then I met your mother!' Sadly, he died in 1975 aged seventy-six. I miss him very much at times.

I mention my parents as they both, in their own way, affect and have relevance to my story. My father by the part of him that is in me, and my mother by her reaction to the events that unfolded in my life.

Following a less than successful academic career at school I eventually scraped into music college. Doubtless, this was because they were short of violinists. Slowly I discovered I was in the wrong place. Two hours of playing for an orchestra in Birmingham Town Hall rehearsing the first four bars of Beethoven's Fifth Symphony, was the pits! I painfully realised that this level of academic intensity was not for me. Popular styles of music appealed far more than the serious stuff. But what do you do to make a living my boy? Music teaching seemed my only option. It was a bad move but it paid the bills. I was never a particularly good educator but I enjoyed the 'out of the classroom stuff'.

I started a folk group which got discovered, signed a recording contract at a London studio called Morgan Music, and in due course left teaching to make my fortune. The folk group in time became a pop group, I learned how to play the violin without the prop of a music sheet in front of me and my keyboard improvisation skills improved tremendously. We played all over the UK in working men's clubs, night clubs and theatres. Also we were the first pop group to tour East Germany. I was now playing electric violin as well as the guitar and electric piano. In Dresden I remember quite vividly performing a love duet with an East German hotel maid called Viola!

Two years as a professional pop musician was invaluable experience. I learned a lot about life and ended up back in teaching, broke, as a failed superstar but having had a bloody good time achieving poverty. With my now much more liberal view of music I started to write musicals for the school that had been kind enough to give me a job. Now this is where it all came together. All my experience seemed ideally suited to this form of music entertainment and I really loved it. I discovered I had the ability to write tunes that kept people awake.

For twelve years this love of the stage musical and writing songs sustained me in a profession I did not really like - the classroom bit again! At times I became so frustrated with this inflexible profession that I took on part time selling jobs, such as encyclopaedias, insurance and double glazing, just to see if I could find another less stressful way to earn my daily crust. My teaching career eventually came to an end when I went to see a doctor, mainly because I was not sleeping well and felt chronic most of the time. It was a doctor I had not seen before.

'What do you do for a living?' he asked.

'I'm a teacher,' I replied.

'Ah! And where do you teach?' he continued.

'In the centre of Birmingham,' I replied.

'Ah h ah!' he said with the air of someone who has just discovered a cure for cancer. 'Get out quick, it's obviously affecting your health!'

Now that was easy to say, but not so easy to do. I had a large mortgage and bills to pay. However a friend of mine suggested doing a C.V. and sending it to all the music companies in the country to see if my knowledge of schools and electronic instruments would be of any use to them. I had one or two polite 'Dear John' replies but only one that invited me for interview. Yamaha were looking for a weird teacher to talk to the weird teachers. I was interviewed and given the job of Education Manager. A terrific six years followed with a company car, expense account, highish salary and trips abroad, all for free. Japan especially was a revelation, not just for their wonderful aural perceptive ways of teaching music to youngsters but also for the very beautiful oriental ladies. My Japanese colleague, however, was always telling me that the ladies in Thailand were the most beautiful he had ever seen. This comment must have lodged itself firmly in my memory, as it would be relevant a few years later. I also learnt how to use a computer to publish music which would also be invaluable to me in the future.

Two years after my father died, around the time I left the pop music business to return to teaching, I got married. This was not to prove a match made in heaven. My mother had warned me, and as usual, I ignored her advice, and as usual, she was right.. How do they do it these mothers? Of course we had our happy times but on the whole the relationship was disastrous. Married in 1978, our daughter Emma was born in 1981 and our son David in 1984. Four years later my wife divorced me, and the children being so young at this time went with her. I was left on my own. The noisy untidy house I lived in was suddenly silent and cold, but still untidy. It was the worst year of my life.

In 1989 we all got back together again and I was now living

in sin with my ex-wife. The sin got less and was replaced by the old familiar destructive arguments. We lived separate lives under the same roof until everyone had had enough. It was decided that the family would split down the middle. David would stay with me and Emma would live with her mother two miles down the road. It was now 1994. The arrangement worked satisfactorily for a few months until my ex-wife found a new partner. He moved in and all hell broke loose. Let's be nice here and call it a clash of personalities! Emma was thirteen and heavily into adolescence. This was not a good time for her to be confronted with yet another difficult situation.

Emma eventually came back to live with me and has slowly been putting her life back together again. I am immensely proud of both my children for the way they handled the many difficulties heaped upon them because of their parents' inability to live with each other.

There is much I have left unsaid about my first marriage. To go into more detail would I feel be one-sided and therefore unfair. When families split up, no-one comes out of it emotionally unscarred.

Talking of emotional scars, remember Yamaha and the great six years? Well they got rid of me. How could they do this? I was irreplaceable! Now known in the Yamaha UK archives as 'Bloody Monday', the company, that day, booted out about twenty other irreplaceable personnel. When the managing director informed me that, sadly, I would have to go, I told him that I felt this could seriously damage my sense of humour. He laughed and asked me if I had any questions. I only had two, how much was the company going to pay me in compensation and how long could I keep the company car? I then cleared my desk and headed back up the motorway for the last time. In my pocket was a cheque for more money than I had ever seen at any one time and a feeling of great freedom that lasted for at least twenty-four hours. That was long enough for me to work out how long seven thousand pounds would actually last me sitting on my bum. I would have to negotiate myself back into teaching. Oh dear, oh dear, oh dear!

Supply teaching is the pits! It is even worse than the first four bars of Beethoven's Fifth! I remember distinctly one incident. I had been at this particular school for about three weeks when the headmistress invited me in for a chat.

'How are you settling in?' she asked with that false, superior smile perfected by heads and politicians.

'I'm not!' I replied with that stare perfected by someone who had just taught 3C and is seriously pissed off.

'Oh,' she said. 'Are you not happy here?'

'No,' I replied. 'Are you?'

Her expression changed. She looked tired and almost human.

'Talk to me,' she said.

'Right, well there have been three very brutal fights in the playground, live bullets found on two children in my classroom, drugs confiscated from at least four pupils, the canteen has been wrecked by a riot and this is only Wednesday! So why should anyone feel happy?'

To be fair, the school was not so very different to many inner city schools. In the six years I had been out of teaching the situation had definitely worsened. Discipline had deteriorated but, more to the point, I had changed. If ever there had been the element of the social worker in me, it had now gone forever. They say, don't they, the wise ones, that you can never go back. There is no worse an animal than a teacher who doesn't really want to teach but the bills still had to be met and supply teaching was not badly paid. Within two months, seriously frustrated, I had decided to start up my own mail order company selling musicals to schools. Fortunately within two years I was able to leave teaching again and rely on the business to sustain me and my children.

Now, six years on, the company is thriving and I am happier being in education but not part of it. I am sure that many teachers and pupils I have known, especially that headmistress, would undoubtedly agree with me that I am better kept out of the classroom!

To take stock, there was I, forty eight years old, divorced, looking after two children, one dog, two cats, two chinchillas, one cockatiel with perfect pitch, working all hours writing and selling musicals.

I decided to take my life by the balls before it was too late and before my remaining teeth and hair dropped out.

Little did I know that this decision to do something with my life was to set me on a road that would eventually take me to the other side of the world and into an adventure greater than anything I had previously encountered.

Departure day for Bangkok eventually dawned. Keith had the job of taking me to Heathrow and Wilf had the job of picking me up two weeks later. It was a lousy morning, typically English, cold, wet and windy. The journey to the airport went by fairly quickly as we were talking all the way about the business and what needed to be done whilst I was away. On reaching the airport we parked the car and walked through to terminal ?. We eventually found the Thai Airways desk where a very helpful lady checked me in. We then went to have a coffee.

Keith noticed that the cup I was holding was shaking. I was suddenly overcome with nerves. What the hell was I doing here? I was going, on my own, to the other side of the world to meet a girl who had written me a letter. I must be bloody crazy! I told Keith I couldn't go. I just wanted to go back home and forget the whole thing. Keith then surprised me. All along he had been very dubious of all this. He had questioned my sanity many times but here, at Heathrow he refused to take me back. He marched me to the passport control doors, and with a very nasty grin on his face, kicked me through them. He always said he would pay me back for getting him involved with teachers! Seriously though, Keith convinced me that I should go. He argued that I definitely needed a holiday and what had I got to lose? It would be a great adventure.

Aladdin's cave lay on the other side of the barrier and it

was all duty free. It took my mind off deliberating about the wisdom of going to Bangkok. I gave in to the British disease of bargain hunting and joined in the melee of people who would board the plane carrying their plastic bags of goodies

Airports held a fascination for me. I spent time people watching and pondered over where they were going and why. Each passenger held a story and the speculation was a mental distraction for me. In the departure lounge, I wondered why all these people were headed for Bangkok. What motivated them? I also wondered if any were looking for a partner, like me.

I sat nursing my apprehensions, my deepest thoughts and my plastic bags full of goodies when the announcement came to board the plane. How big this monster was! How did they ever get off the ground? I was impressed by man's ingenuity as I made my way to the rear section of the aircraft reserved for smokers.

The stewardesses were all the agency had foretold they would be, beautiful Thai ladies who moved with more grace and femininity than I had ever encountered before. The stewardess who was serving our section of the plane was, in my opinion, the most attractive.

She was so kind to me, so attentive, and her smile was warm and inviting. She obviously fancied me and by the time we took off I was in love. I watched her for the first hour of the flight and soon discovered that she was just as warm and attentive to everyone in our section, male or female. I had learned my first valuable lesson. Thais have a lovely way of making you feel attractive; it's the way they smile. This does not mean, however, that they find you irresistible and want to rip your trousers off - shame really.

Six hours later we were crossing India. I peered through the confines of the window and looked down six or seven miles to the great sub-continent. The land mass was a brown furze with no distinguishable features. From this height what could I expect? I delved into the recesses of schoolday memory and conjured pictures of exotic spices, silks and elephants and the great masses of a third world hauling itself painfully into the twentieth century. But I could not identify anything to satisfy this image. All the land masses looked the same from up here. Of the seething millions of souls I could see nothing, but they were there and so were the elephants, I felt sure. I was then distracted by the return of my favourite stewardess, now in traditional Thai costume, and I smiled my warmest smile.

Eight hours into the flight I was not quite so keen on flying anymore. I hadn't been able to sleep, my back ached and I just wished we were there. Then I must have fallen asleep because the next thing I remember was someone shaking me asking for a pair of headphones. I stirred as the whisper of the stewardess breathed past me, the faintest smell of discreetly exotic blooms wafted over me. Oh to be woken every morning by such a fragrance.

Only thirty minutes to go - wonderful - just time for a cup of tea. Then, fasten your seat belts, put out your fags, bumpety bump and I had arrived in Bangkok.

And so full of over optimistic eastern promise I entered the hotel where I now sat, ten days later, a dejected and unhappy man.

The past and present whirled around my brain. I was exhausted. No doubt of that. The roller coaster ride had suddenly come up against a brick wall and I felt dazed with the collision. The thoughts of the known past were real, they had happened. I could relate to all that had led me to my being here but since then I had somehow lost my way, lost control. I was experiencing murderous thoughts against Fagin. Most of all I was angry with myself. Nobody likes to admit they have been foolish but I had to face it. This whole thing had been a total disaster. The happiness and companionship I was looking for had receded into the distance and had now gone from sight with the departure of the tearful Lisa. I was going to look a right fool when I eventually got back to England. The only saving grace was that I could say I had needed a break and had enjoyed the holiday but this was not what I came here for and my family and friends all knew that. I would just have to brazen it out and save face as best I could.

Beads of sweat rolled down the familiar pathway of my spine and settled in the emptiness of my being.

That evening I saw Martin sitting in reception and related the events of the past few days. His opinion of the agency was even lower than mine. He'd also had some bad experiences with them and agreed with me that they were not to be trusted and best avoided. He was now fairly convinced that Ning Nong had been a plant by the agency and that she actually had no intention of marrying him, or any western man. He felt that Clive had been very lucky to meet a genuine girl like Karla via the agency.

Martin had much to say about Clive's wedding. He waxed lyrical on the subject of Buddhist ceremonies with their mystical traditions and colourful spectacle. He had obviously enjoyed the whole experience but though I listened politely, little of what he had to say penetrated the barriers of my own personal misery, and was lost on me.

Clive was in his room with his new bride as they had to attend the British Embassy very early the next day to apply for a settlement visa so that Karla could return to England with her husband. The agency had indicated all along that this would be a formality as long as the man could show sufficient funds to support his new wife. So it was assumed that Clive wouldn't have a problem. Wrong!

The next morning reception saw two very sad people. The Embassy had failed their application for a visa using the Primary Purpose law. This law basically gives the Embassy the right of opinion. They interview both parties and even if all the paperwork is in order, they can refuse a visa on grounds that, in their opinion, the girl's main purpose for wanting to go to England is not primarily the desire to be with her husband. That's all they were told. Clive apparently begged them to reverse their decision, but to no avail. They would now have the option to reapply to the British Embassy in Bangkok, where they would have to show some change in circumstances. Or alternatively they could appeal against the ruling, which takes a long time but the case would then be heard back in England. The latter was thought to be their best option as being in England Clive could more easily seek legal help and advice. They were both obviously very distraught. To go from the elation of the Buddhist ceremony to the realisation that Clive would now have to leave Karla in Bangkok, with no real idea of when he would be able to return, was devastating for both of them. This was my first encounter with the Primary Purpose Law. Fagin was duly informed of their failure to get a visa to which he replied,

'You'll just have to get her pregnant. The child would be a British citizen and then they would have to give you a visa.'

Now there's the Christian spirit going at full blast! The man wasn't just bad - he was evil!

All that Martin and I could do was commiserate and offer our full support to them both.

Clive and Martin then left the hotel to visit a Thai lawyer who they thought might have some ideas in relation to getting Karla a visa. This was to be a long shot, and didn't in the end achieve anything for Clive. It did however achieve something for Martin. The lawyer also ran a marriage agency as a side line and introduced Martin to a Thai lady called Gow.

So Martin was happy, I was still depressed, and Clive was suicidal.

5. Why me? Why not?

I had breakfast with a little pixie faced Irishman called Dan. He was a tax inspector, lived in Dublin, and had been in Bangkok for the past three weeks. In that time, via the agency, he had met about twenty ladies, been out with ten, been accepted by three, and had chosen one. He'd obviously read the same American sales technique book I had!

Dan was amazing. He'd approached this whole thing mathematically. He had made notes on each of the twenty ladies he initially interviewed, whittled the list down to ten that he took out on a date. He then picked three for a second date, and made his choice. Unfortunately he had come unstuck when he tried to convince the chosen lady's parents that the bride price was better paid by instalments over three years. He was travelling back to Dublin the following day with very little money left, but having kept his dry Irish sense of humour fully intact. I liked him very much, and talking to him cheered me up a lot.

Following my chat with Dan I was sitting in reception, pondering whether it took as much electricity to keep cool as it took to keep warm, when Martin emerged from the hotel lift. He walked across to where I was sitting and asked if I fancied going shopping as he had some presents to buy. I also needed to buy the odd gift and so we hit the roadside traders on the Sukhumvit Road, the great six lane artery of Bangkok. Martin was a lot better than I at the bartering, he'd had a lot more practice, so I told him what I wanted and he got it all at a reasonable price. The Sukhumvit has shops on either side. In between the shops and the road there is a fairly wide pavement. Some time ago this pavement was dug up to lay cables for telephones but they were never replaced again properly and so the area is an obstacle course, milling with western shoppers all tripping up. On this very uneven pavement are market traders selling the typical tourist stuff. The prices are very low, compared to the west, and by bartering you could reduce the asking price by as much as fifty per cent.

Martin was very good at this and we spent a happy couple of hours trying to convince hard-nosed Thai traders that we were poverty stricken westerners. Two hours is a long time to be outside on the Sukhumvit Road with the heat and the pollution so we decided to go somewhere for a cooling drink. Martin suggested a nearby hotel called The Landmark, the one I had spotted from the window of my room. We walked down a very long staircase adjacent to the Sukhumvit Road, through a small underground shopping arcade and into The Huntsman Pub, as it was called. I was thankful for the air conditioning in The Huntsman. It was wonderfully cool, spacious and looked typically American in style. In one corner a small stage with drums and amplifiers indicated that live bands played there, while on the other side of the central bar island there was a very large T.V. showing pop videos.

We sat at a table on the left hand side of the large central bar area. Martin ordered us a couple of Singha beers from one of the gorgeous waitresses in a long mauve dress. We sipped the iced beer gratefully and chatted about our experiences with the street traders. I was feeling somewhat better having snapped out of my earlier doldrums. A hand appeared from over my shoulder and the glasses were dutifully topped up.

'Thank you very much,' I said without looking up.
'You are welcome, Sir,' a voice replied.
Something in the voice made me turn. I looked up. Somewhere inside me a butterfly took wing. To say she was lovely was an understatement. In a city full of lovely girls she would stand out like the palace over the rooftops. Somehow the babble of the voices, the pop video and the distant rumble of traffic on the Sukhumvit Road faded into nothingness. For a few seconds there was an invisible aura that connected her to me. I was then aware of Martin's voice which jolted me grudgingly back to reality. The noises returned and the buzzing in my head cleared. The butterfly was still again.

I smiled at her as she topped up Martin's glass. She smiled back, exchanged our ashtray for a clean one and went over to the bar area.

I looked at Martin who laughed. He had read my mind and said that to get to know a girl like this would take a long time. In his experience it would mean coming in here every day for the next few weeks, sitting at the same table, being very attentive to her, always to have one beer and then a coffee so that she did not think I was a heavy drinker, never to be seen looking intently at any of the other girls, and, in time, to ask her to go for a meal but with some of her friends so that she would feel secure. But I was leaving in two days! I hadn't got the time to go through all that stuff! She returned to our table and with the same velvet voice asked if we would like some more drink. I ordered another beer for Martin, a coffee for me, and asked her name.

'Warune, but everyone calls me Whisky, sir.'

'Why Whisky? I asked smiling.

'The Thai name Warune means whisky for the Angels, Sir.'

'I didn't know that Angels drank whisky, Whisky.'

'They probably don't, sir,' she replied, giggled and walked back to her station.

'Martin my boy. I have to get to know this girl!'

'You've got no chance Mike, she's engaged.' Martin said emphatically.

He had noticed a gold bracelet on her wrist which usually indicates the same thing as an engagement ring in the west. My heart sank. I was on a roller coaster again. I had to know. In fact there was suddenly helluva lot I wanted to know about this girl. I simply did not have the time to obey conventions. I was going back to England in two days time. My world stood on it's head.

When she returned to our table, I pointed to the bracelet and asked if she was engaged. She smiled, looked at me very discerningly, and walked away after changing our ashtray yet again.

'You've really embarrassed her now and completely blown it,' said Martin, content in the fact that he was being proved right.

As she passed our table the next time she smiled, crouched

to the level of my ear, pointed to the bracelet and said very softly,

'I bought it myself, sir.'

All this was obviously too much for Martin who retired, confused, to the toilet. Whisky returned and asked again if we required anything else to drink. I replied that we unfortunately had to go and asked for the bill, which she duly brought over. This was it! Have confidence Mike. Go for it! I looked straight into her eyes and said I thought she was a very beautiful lady and that I would very much like to get to know her. I told her that I was returning to England in a couple of days but would like to write to her. Would she be willing to write back? She looked very puzzled and said,

'Why me, Sir?'

I smiled and replied, 'Why not Whisky?' She giggled again.

'But you are an attractive man, sir. You must have many ladies,' she said.

'Whisky,' I said shaking my head, 'if you knew the story of my life over the past few years you would realise just how funny that statement is.' She looked puzzled again.

'I would very much like to tell you about myself and please believe my sincerity, I really would like to get to know you Whisky. Will you write to me if I write to you?' She looked at me with a very serious expression on her face, and there was one of those silences that seems to last for ages. She then broke the tension with a smile and said,

'Okay sir. Thank you very much.'

I promised to return the following day with a letter for her containing my address. I said goodbye and joined Martin who was waiting patiently for me outside the pub. If I remember correctly I jumped up and punched the air with my fist. After all, I'd just scored a goal in extra time! Yes!

Martin said he was amazed and had never seen anything like it in all his travels.

'In my opinion Mike she has probably agreed to write to get rid of you politely. Let's face it, she's gorgeous. She must be chatted up every day by eager western punters who tend to think that all female flesh in Bangkok is available. That's why respectable Thai ladies are so hard to get to know. They have a very low opinion of men, especially western men.'

I listened to his very logical opinion of my first encounter with Whisky but he hadn't been there in that moment of silence when she looked at me so deeply. I knew something had passed between us. I was fairly sure it was not just my imagination going berserk. However I have been known to be wrong in the past and was about to go through a very long twenty-four hours waiting to find out. It suddenly occurred to me that I didn't know for sure that she would even be at work the next day.

That evening saw me slaving over a letter that just had to be right in its content. I had just met the most sensational woman. A door had suddenly appeared from nowhere and opened for me. I saw an opportunity, a chance perhaps. I wanted her to get to know me, and I had so little time. What could I say? Above all it was important that she be left in no doubt as to the sincerity of my intentions. This was not going to be easy and as the hours went by the waste bin filled to overflowing with my failed attempts. I did not want to sound like some love-sick playboy gushing out his inner emotions. No, I must stick to the facts. Tell her something about myself - cards on the table right from the start. I tried again and again. Finally I was satisfied. It was the best I could do. I had simply told her who I was, what I did for a living and about my children and divorce. It was honest, forthright and factual. Finally I asked her if she would be kind enough to go out for a meal with me on the Sunday evening after she had finished work and suggested she bring a friend. Tired, and full of anticipation, I went to bed.

The next morning I rewrote the letter so that it was more legible and hoped that Whisky's ability to read English was as good as her spoken English. Around twelve o'clock midday I returned to The Landmark and entered The Huntsman Pub. Whisky was at her station with her back to me. I walked across to her and said hello. She looked very surprised to see me and I handed her the letter which she put quickly into her apron pocket. She showed me to a table and offered me a beer. I accepted. As I drank the beer she was flitting in and out of the service doors and I presumed she was reading my letter out of the gaze of whoever was her superior. Eventually she came over to my table again and asked if I wanted another beer. I asked for a coffee and inquired if she had read the letter yet. She giggled and walked away. This scene was repeated three times with three coffees and three giggles. She returned to the table once again and I asked her what her answer was regarding the meal and assured her that I was going to sit there drinking coffee until she said yes. She laughed and said,

'Okay Mike. The answer is yes.'

We arranged to meet outside The Landmark at seven o'clock that evening. Within the space of twenty-four hours, I had gone from the depths of despair to the heights of elation and from the earnest desire to get back home to the frustration of having to leave Bangkok the next day. Why is my life never simple? On returning to the hotel, I found Clive and Martin in reception checking out. We sat down together to have a final coffee and a chat while they waited for their taxi to arrive. Clive was in very low spirits. Karla was by his side and had obviously been crying. It was all very sad. Their marriage would now have to undergo separation before it had really been given a chance to get started. I promised him I would telephone as soon as I arrived back in England so that we could arrange to get together. Clive was going to need a lot of understanding and support back in the UK. Martin seemed quite happy with his new lady Gow and was talking about returning to Bangkok fairly soon.

Eventually the taxi arrived and we all said our goodbyes, for the moment anyway. They all wished me luck with Whisky and left for the airport.

That evening, I decided to get a taxi from my hotel to The Landmark. It was a journey of only half a mile at the most but it was now drizzling with rain and I vainly wanted to look my best. As I climbed out of the taxi I saw Whisky waiting about one hundred yards up the road from The Landmark entrance. She waved. I waved back, paid the driver and walked up to where she was standing. Whisky looked stunning in a dark blue trouser suit. With a radiant smile she said hello and introduced me to her girlfriend from work and her friend's brother, whose names I don't recall. Whisky opened the large umbrella she was carrying, positioned it over my head and we started to walk side by side down the Sukhumvit Road. The restaurant fortunately was only a short distance away. It was small and did not look expensive. We entered and were shown to a table for four. I sat next to Whisky and her friends sat opposite. I can't remember what we ate, except that it was a Thai dish chosen by Whisky. Her friends insisted on wanting only an ice-cream each. We all chatted away and with each passing minute I was becoming more and more convinced that I had found the girl I had so long been looking for. She was wonderful, so full of spirit and fun. She only had to look at me and I melted. She seemed to find me amusing because she laughed a lot at the things I said, but I didn't find out very much about her on this first date. Very cleverly, she kept the conversation wound around me, my circumstances, my children and England. She was very inquisitive and asked a lot of questions. Her friends didn't say much as their English was limited. Suddenly Whisky said that she would have to go because she had a long journey back to her home. I commented that I hadn't had my ice cream yet as a ploy to get her to stay longer. Whisky laughed, apologised and promised to buy me an ice cream if ever we saw each other again.

'Would you like to see me again Whisky?' I asked quickly.

'Yes of course, why not' she replied.

Outside the restaurant we said goodnight to her friends and walked together back up the Sukhumvit Road to hail a taxi. I offered to go with her but she said very firmly that it was not such a good idea. I asked her if she would join me the next day after work for a quick drink before I left for the airport. She said she thought that would be lovely, thanked me for the meal, stepped into a taxi and waved to me as it sped away into the night, still with that lovely smile on her face.

I walked slowly back to the hotel in a bit of a daze. I had known many girls in my life, but never, ever, had I felt like this. My mind was racing. How soon could I get back to Bangkok? How was I going to afford to return? Would my ex-wife be willing to look after the kids again? Would Keith continue to be supportive, and would my mother really leave all her money to the dogs' home? These, and other questions about the meaning of life, successfully kept me awake again into the early hours of the morning when exhaustion finally won and I slept.

This was the best night's sleep I'd had since my arrival and I awoke at noon, invigorated, and with a Spring chicken feeling in my legs. I went, naturally to have lunch at The Huntsman. The place was packed and Whisky was very busy so we had little opportunity to talk but I arranged to meet her outside The Landmark at six-thirty.

I headed to the shops to buy Whisky a present but what should I get for a beautiful woman I had only just met? I didn't want to go over the top in case she thought I was trying to impress her with so called Western wealth. Remembering something Martin had said about Cadbury's chocolate being an expensive luxury in Thailand, I bought a large block of Fruit and Nut. I also purchased a book about Great Britain full of wonderful photographs. Like bait, I attached these items to my romantic fishing line and to add weight, I returned to my hotel to write another letter to explain to Whisky that I would be returning to Bangkok as soon as possible so that we could get to know each other better. I raised my hopes higher as the few remaining hours and minutes of my time ticked away.

That evening saw me outside The Landmark at six thirty waiting for Whisky. I had packed already so that all I had to do later was pick up my cases and get a taxi to the airport. I would have to leave the hotel by nine o'clock to be sure of arriving at the airport on time. So I had two hours to spend with Whisky.

Oh no I didn't! Things went wrong. Six forty five, no Whisky, seven o'clock, no Whisky. Throughout the time I was waiting a

Thai guy was constantly pestering me to have a look at his little picture book of available ladies of the night. In the end I had to tell him to piss off as he just wouldn't take no for an answer. I walked down the long staircase that led to the arcade and up to the entrance of the Huntsman Pub. I couldn't see Whisky and asked the girl on the door if Miss Warune was still there. She replied, 'Miss Warune go home already, sir.' My stomach did a somersault. I gave her the bag of goodies and asked her if she would give them to Whisky the following day. She kindly said that she would do so. Back out on The Sukhumvit, feeling really deflated, I waited until seven fifteen just in case. But she didn't show. You foolish little man, I thought, how could you have believed that a lady as young and gorgeous as Whisky could possibly be interested in you? I started to walk back to the hotel feeling utterly dejected. On my way I saw a female figure in front of me walking very slowly. It looked just like Whisky from the back. I drew level with her. It was Whisky.

'I've been waiting for you outside The Landmark for nearly an hour. Where were you?' I asked.

'I know,' she replied. 'I was watching you. We go now.' She quickened her pace and I walked beside her. Nothing was said until we entered an ice cream parlour fairly near by.

'I buy you ice cream I promised,' she said, smiling as she extracted some money from the back pocket of her blue jeans. I don't know if Whisky was able to see the intense relief my face must have been showing, but intensely relieved I certainly was. She brought the ice cream over to me, sat down, and then explained that she could not be seen with a western man outside the hotel in which she worked. All was now clear, except for wondering why I hadn't been instructed to meet her elsewhere.

I now discovered a little more about her. She was twenty four years old and had two younger sisters. She had worked at The Landmark for about one year and wanted to do well to achieve promotion. She studied English at the hotel which ran a course for their staff and she didn't have a boyfriend. Good news, or what! She also told me that her mother was a cook and worked very, very hard. For my part I think I probably over did it slightly trying to assure her of my honourable intentions. I just had to convince her that I wasn't just another bull-shitter from the west. She told me that she had been asked out to dinner many times by western men but that the previous night was the first time she had accepted. I asked her why then had she said yes to me? At which she shrugged her shoulders, looked very deeply into my eyes and said,

'Not sure really.'

Whisky then took her serviette, dabbed her lips with it, and placed it on the table. I picked up the serviette, kissed the impression her lips had made, folded it, and put it into my shirt pocket.

'Mike, I think you smooth talker,' Whisky said, looking at me very intently.

'You mean you're not impressed,' I said, smiling. 'That's a shame because it worked well in a film I saw recently.'

Whisky laughed. 'You never serious Mike, you always joking,' she said.

'I like to make you laugh, it's good to laugh. But I'm very serious about one thing, Whisky, I will be back.' I enunciated every syllable. 'I want to get to know you better. Please believe me, I will be back.' I meant every word but the thought did cross my mind that I must have sounded like Swarzenegger.

Sadly, it was then time for me to go. Outside the parlour I told her about the bag of goodies and letter I had left back at The Huntsman. I held her hand and again assured her I would return, if she would like me to. She said she would and promised to reply to my letters. With that established I kissed her on the cheek. She looked very embarrassed and said that she didn't think she would sleep well that night. I looked straight into her eyes and yet again assured her that nothing would now stop me returning to Bangkok. I turned and started to walk back to the hotel, holding back a tear. A little cute, soft spoken voice behind me said,

'Goodbye sir.'

I turned, waved, and took one last look at her very

beautiful, yet enigmatic face.

On the way back to the hotel I passed a roadside stall displaying glittering effigies and brilliantly coloured fabrics, all showing the face and the form of Buddha. As I looked they all seemed to smile at me in a silent chorus. Wistfully, I smiled back.

6. Back to England

Bangkok International Airport was very busy that Monday night and so checking in took ages. I don't think I have ever felt so alone surrounded by so many people. I just didn't want to be there. I wanted to be back with Whisky. There were already a thousand questions in my head that I wanted to ask her, but they would all have to wait.

As I sat waiting in the departure lounge, with all the other western passengers, the Thai air hostesses walked in. Every man's head turned to look and every woman looked depressed. It was a look I was becoming used to. It was a look of frustration. It summed up my initial reason for being here in Bangkok. The western women who sat around me were, on the whole, frumpy, shabbily dressed and not at all feminine. There was no comparison to the slim, elegant, feminine air hostesses that had just walked in. Somewhere along the line western ladies had lost it. I know this is a big generalisation, but where was the grace, the softness, the femininity that western ladies used to possess? I had looked very hard for it in England and had to travel seven thousand miles to find it in abundance. I would, over the forthcoming months, have many discussions with western men on this subject, the vast majority agreeing with my perceptions. Beauty of course, is only skin deep and I had a lot to learn about the beauty that lay behind the Thai eyes. At this point in my life, with the experience I had, for better or for worse, that was my view.

The flight back was uneventful. Every time the air hostess asked me if I wanted a drink I felt obliged to have a whisky - obvious really. After about three hours and five or six

As I emerged from customs at Heathrow Airport I saw my good friend Wilf's friendly face beaming at me from the other side of the barrier. We went to have a cup of good old English tea before hitting the motorway back home to the midlands.

I told Wilf all about my trip and the events that had unfolded. He listened silently and attentively to my story.

'So basically it's like this Mick,' he said. Wilf always calls me Mick because he knows it annoys me. He's that sort of friend.

'You've been all the way to the Bangkok?'

'Yes Wilf.'

'The sex capital of the eastern world?'

'Yes Wilf.'

'You've spent a lot of money Mick?'

'Yes Wilf.'

'Which you can't afford?'

'Very true Wilf.'

'And you've come back celibate?'

'Yes Wilf.'

'Well I think you're off your bleedin' head Mick!'

'Thank you Wilf.'

With that my very good and supportive friend drove me back to my home, trying all the way to convince me that, in his considered opinion, I would be crazy to return to Bangkok.

'You know nothing about this girl, Mick.'

'That's why I need to go back there Wilf.'

'She might have Aids or something Mick. That Bangkok's a very funny place.'

'Don't be silly Wilf, she's a very respectable lady.'

'But you don't know for sure, do you Mick?'

'No Wilf, that's why I'm going back!'

Round and round in circles we went, all the way home. Be assured though, agree with me or disagree with me, Wilf would always be there for me, as he had always been in the past. In the year I had spent on my own following divorce Wilf was as good a friend as anyone could wish for. He came to see me regularly and his technique of dealing with my emotional dilemma was enviable, although I didn't realise it at the time.

If I was relating how terrible my ex-wife was, Wilf would

agree with me.

'I know Mick, she really was a difficult lady. You don't de-serve to be treated like that. I think you're well rid pal!'

If I was feeling low and missing my ex-wife and children Wilf would say things like,

'It's all very sad Mick, she wasn't a bad old stick you know.'

At a party recently where I was telling someone how well I had coped with that period of my life Wilf jumped down my throat,

'Coped well! What do you mean, coped well! You were a complete and utter pain in the arse. I know, I was there. I was just eternally grateful she came back and I didn't have to listen to you crapping on any more!'

We arrived at my home just before noon to find good old Keith slaving away at the computer logging the orders received that day.

'Well was it an adventure?' he asked.

'It sure bloody was, my friend!' I replied.

I had to recount the events of the last two weeks again for Keith, and Wilf sat through it a second time.

'I still say you're off your head Mick!' he repeated. 'I couldn't do it. No way Hose!'

With that Wilf left to go home to his wife Margy, leaving me to the tender mercies of Keith who, in no uncertain terms, told me that if I did go back to Bangkok he would have to have help to run the company.

It took about two hours for Keith to bring me up to date with business matters and then he left. I was on my own. I sat down and wrote my first letter to Whisky. I hadn't even unpacked. Suddenly it was time to pick up the kids from school. They very pleased to see me and wanted to know what I had bought them, typical!

For the third time that day I found myself relating the whole story. Already it seemed so far away. The kids asked me if I had any photographs and suddenly I realised I hadn't got a picture of Whisky. 'Why hadn't I got one?' I cursed myself. It suddenly became so obviously important to me too. I unsealed the envelope which held my letter to Whisky and added a postscript requesting her to send me a photograph to show my children.

It was good to be back home, to be with my kids but my thoughts were in far away Bangkok which seemed another world and the gap of seven thousand miles grew longer in my thoughts. I wrote to Whisky every other day. My letters were factual about me, my children and my past. I told her too my hopes for the future. I sent photos of everything, the children, the house, even the car and our pets. I wanted to give her as full an impression of me and my life, so that even though we were apart, she would learn a lot more about me. Desperately I wanted to hear her voice but was reluctant to telephone her at work in case she was not allowed to receive personal calls. I sat down and composed a tune and sent it to her on cassette tape. It was a slushy romantic instrumental piece I called 'Whisky's Song' naturally. My door-mat, however, remained empty. The bills, as usual, arrived as did the business mail, but no letter from Whisky.

During this time Clive and I were talking to each other fairly regularly on the telephone. My frustration was nothing compared to what he was going through. Karla had been very badly affected by their failure to get a visa. She felt that it was all her fault. She had kept repeating to Clive, as he was waiting to leave the airport in Bangkok, 'Am fail, Am fail.' He kept reassuring her that she hadn't failed anything and that it was the British Embassy who had failed to recognise their genuine request for a visa. It was all of course very, very sad and the future was now very uncertain for them both.

Selfishly, the thing that made my situation worse at this time was the fact that Karla wrote to Clive at least twice a week. She wrote her letters in Thai and Clive had to have them translated. Then he wrote back in English, had the letter translated into Thai, and posted it. A lot of hassle it may well have been, but at least he wasn't staring at an empty door mat every morning. I even sent Whisky a photograph of my empty doormat to see if humour might hasten a response, but still no letter arrived.

Clive said he thought I should telephone. After four weeks of no letters, what had I got to lose? Let's face it, I didn't even know for sure that Whisky had received any of my letters.

So I took the bull by the horns and telephoned The Landmark. I was really nervous. The operator at the hotel put me straight through to The Huntsman Pub where a female voice answered in Thai. I asked, in English, if I could speak to Miss Warune. The line went silent. Suddenly I heard Whisky's voice.
'Hello, Warune speak.'
'Hi Whisky,' I replied. 'It's Mike.'

Her voice sounded elated. She was happy to hear from me. We exchanged pleasantries regarding her mother and work and I told her I missed her very much. She said she was missing me too. I told her I would be returning to Bangkok. She wanted to know when. I said I was not sure but to believe it would be soon.

I asked her if she had received my letters. She had, and thought they were lovely. She apologised for not yet having replied but she was busy at work and when she got home she was too tired to write a letter in English as it took a lot of concentration. She assured me she had started a letter and would finish it soon and post it to me. She wanted me to come back to see her as soon as I could as she really did miss me. I promised I would and that I would telephone her again in a few days time now that I knew it was okay to do so. Then we said our goodbyes.

I stared at the telephone for ages. I was elated with her reaction but troubled about the fact that, in four weeks, she hadn't completed a letter to me.

My kids were very supportive. Nearly every day Emma asked me if I'd received a letter from Whisky. Inwardly I screamed!

Two more weeks went by, and still no letter! Lots of telephone conversations with Whisky, all very pleasant, all assuring me I was being missed but still no letter. I even sent flowers via Interfloral

Then at last she said that the letter was finished. It must have been the flowers that cracked it! Oh deep joy, I was going at last to receive a letter.

No I wasn't! Another week went by with the same annoyingly empty doormat. Now I was angry. Oh boy was I angry. She said she had written the letter, so why hadn't I received the letter?

The answer was quite simple. She hadn't posted it! Her excuse again was pressure of work but the truth finally emerged. She was embarrassed by her written English and her inability to write a letter accurately.

'Your letters are so good Mike,' she said. 'I do not know what to write to you about. My life is so boring.'

I kicked myself for my failure to see the obvious. I just wanted to be by her side to reassure her that any letter she wrote to me, no matter how inadequate she thought it was, would be the best letter I had ever received. But I was on the end of a seven thousand mile telephone line. I told her to not worry about it and write to me in Thai then I would, like Clive, have it translated. She promised me that she would post the letter the following day and asked me to please excuse her bad English. She asked me again when I would be going back to Thailand.

It was now well into December, and the rehearsals for the local pantomime were well under way. There was no chance of my returning to Bangkok until after the show in late January.

A few days before Christmas Whisky's letter finally arrived. As I came down stairs that morning I saw a little blue air mail envelope sitting on my previously lonely doormat. I jumped down the last four stairs, opened the envelope and took out the single page letter, it read as follows:

Dear Mike,

How are you now? Thank you very mush for your lovely gift. I am grateful that I have someone who are very kind to me. How very thoughtful of you? I got a surprise when I opened the bag. I met something very special to me 'Whisky song'I enjoy it and I never feel bored.
I'm always wrong in English. It is a difficult language for me. I know I'm not so good English, but everyday I try to practise to speak but I always wrong.
If you come back to Thailand again I'd like you to teach me English I will be good student. And the end I have got nothing to give you excep my thinkness and my picture.
I make up my mind to wait for you here. I hope you will be back again.
I miss you too. I'm looking forward to seeing you in January.

Whisky

I thought the letter was damn good for someone with no confidence in their ability. And I was right. It was the best letter I had ever received and I now had a photograph to show the kids. Both Emma and David thought Whisky looked beautiful.

Clive thought that the line 'I make up my mind to wait for you here' held great significance. In his opinion it meant Whisky was confirming that I was now her boyfriend and because Thai ladies are very loyal I had nothing to worry about. I picked up the telephone and booked my air ticket.

7. The First Return of the Englishman

'So throw this past me again will you Mick?'

'Yes Wilf.'

'You're going back to Bangkok?'

'Yes Wilf.'

'The last time you went, you, and everyone else, thought it bloody crazy to travel to the other side of the world to meet a girl that had only written you one letter?'

'Yes Wilf.'

'How many letters has Whisky written you Mick?'

'One Wilf.'

'Well I'm sorry Mick, you've lost me here somewhere. Far be it for me to state the obvious, but what's the difference?'

'Look Wilf,' I replied. 'Don't worry, this is different. You haven't met Whisky. She's special.'

'Oh come on Mick, they're all bloody special, till you marry 'em that is.'

'That's a bit cynical Wilf.'

'I don't care Mick, it's got to be said. Your 'ead ain't straight! You're ravin' mad pal! You're up a tree with this thing! I don't know why you don't try to find a nice English girl. It'd be a lot cheaper!'

Wilf is a character. Born and bred in the Black Country. In his own words,

'The way I look at it Mick is this, if you can't get on with me you've got a problem!'

And he's probably about right in that assessment.

It has to be said that at this time he did his very best to stop me going back to Bangkok. All with the best of intentions of course. He really believed I was 'up a tree' and would get badly burned.

Before I returned to Bangkok I visited Clive in Wrexham. It was just so good to talk to someone who understood completely why I was going back to Thailand. On the whole he was coping quite well with the forced separation from Karla. He had started to find out many things about the appeal procedure, and although he now knew for sure that it would be a fairly long drawn out process, he felt better for doing something. It must have been terrible for Karla in Thailand who could do nothing but wait. She was still writing lots of letters to Clive which spurred him on in his endeavours to reverse the decision of the Embassy in Bangkok. He had also made a decision to learn to speak Thai. This was to be no easy task as it's an extremely difficult language to learn but as Karla did not speak any English, it seemed to Clive the logical thing to do. He loved her and had married her, but he didn't really know her that well.

I was happy to see him so positive and we spent a lovely weekend together chatting about all things Thai. He showed me all of Karla's letters, a substantial pile to be sure compared to the one letter I had received from Whisky. His house was like a shrine dedicated to Karla. There were large photographs of her everywhere and lots of Thai ornaments decorating the odd shelf. I finally left after discussing the possibility of a joint trip to Thailand later in the year, assuming that my forthcoming two weeks with Whisky went well.

A week later I was on my way to Bangkok, this time with KLM via Amsterdam as it was a much cheaper fare. It put about three hours on to the travelling time but nevertheless an excellent flight.

Whisky had booked me a room at a small, inexpensive hotel within five minutes walking distance of The Landmark. She had told me that she would try to get some days off work so that we could spend as much time together as possible.

Back in Wrexham Clive had given me the benefit of his experience. He'd read a lot about Thai ways and customs, and so I listened very attentively to all that he had to say. To me Clive was an expert, after all he'd been to Bangkok twice!

He told me that when Whisky met me at the airport, she would be all dressed up, probably be with family and friends, and would definitely have a little spray of flowers for me. I would need to take great note of how she greeted me, how high was the Wai. I would have to respond with a Wai of equal height. We would then got into a taxi, go to the hotel where she would see me checked in and wait for me in reception. Under no circumstances did he think that she would go up to my room with me. He said that I should have a small gift ready to give her and other smaller gifts for her family and friends. He emphasised that this was a big event for Whisky. A man was travelling seven thousand miles to see her and she would want to impress me with Thai custom and hospitality.

Wrong! Wrong! Wrong! Whisky was obviously not a typical Thai.

Yes, she was waiting at the airport, but on her own dressed in jeans and a tee-shirt. There were no flowers, no family or friends, and no Wai. She just said,

'Hi Mike. How are you?' and we went to book a taxi.

On the way to the hotel Whisky was full of questions about my children. She made no mention of the romantic content of my correspondence, she wanted to talk about the children and so we did. Whisky thought that Emma was very beautiful and David very cute. I was just so happy to be with her again.

Suddenly, as we approached The Landmark Hotel, Whisky gave out a little yelp, fell to her knees on to the floor of the taxi, and covered her head with my jacket.

'What on earth are you doing Whisky?' I asked.

'Captain walk on Sukhumvit. Must not see,' she replied.

The captain she referred to was apparently her superior at work and for some reason Whisky did not want to be seen. Before I could extract any further information we were at the hotel, and she was still on the floor of the taxi.

Inside the hotel she stood by me while I checked in, carried one of my suitcases to the lift, got into the lift with me, came into my room with me, and started to unpack for me. So much for all

Clive's books on Thai customs! This Thai girl had obviously not read them.

While she unpacked she insisted that I have a shower. Having completed this task, and smelling sweetly, I sat on the edge of the bed where Whisky joined me and we chatted for about an hour. No kissing, no cuddling, we just held hands and chatted. It felt wonderful, I was on cloud nine. But not for long.

It was now about three o'clock in the afternoon and Whisky announced that she had to go shopping with her mother.

'You've got to go where?' I asked, utterly deflated.

'Shopping with my mother Mike.'

'But Whisky, I've just travelled seven thousand miles to see you. Couldn't you go shopping with your mother next week?'

She laughed and said, 'Look Mike you very tired, you must rest and will see you tomorrow.'

'No I'm not tired and I don't need to rest,' I fired back. 'And what am I going to do on my own until tomorrow? I don't know anybody in this city except you.'

She smiled sweetly, 'Mike, you're in Bangkok. There's lots to do. It's a very exciting place, I'm sure you won't be lonely.'

'What on earth do you mean by that Whisky? I don't understand.'

'Mike, I have to go. Just enjoy yourself. I don't mind, really.' she said, picking up her bag in readiness to leave.

'Whisky, I'm not here to enjoy myself, I'm here to get to know you.'

She really laughed at this last desperate comment, kissed me on the cheek, and left.

I know her little game, I thought. She wants to see if I go off with any bar girls. That's what she thinks all western men do in Bangkok. She'll be back tomorrow with loads of questions. Where did you go? What did you do? Typical woman!

Anyway she was right about one thing. I was feeling tired, so I had a little sleep. Seven hours of little sleep in actual fact. When I awoke it was ten thirty at night and I was very hungry. I ventured downstairs to the hotel restaurant and had a meal that wasn't half bad. I bought a book from reception, returned to my room, and started to read. I'll show her, I thought. I'll just stay in my hotel room until she returns. That will really confuse her.

So stay in my room I did and finished the book by twelve noon the following day, but still no Whisky. I went down to the restaurant again to have some lunch. Still no Whisky.

Back in my room at three o'clock in the afternoon the telephone on the bedside table rang. I leapt off the bed and picked up the receiver. It was reception informing me that Miss Warune had arrived. I asked them to send her up. Now keep calm, I said to myself, don't lose your cool. It was obviously a very long shopping trip.

As I opened the door to let her in she flung her arms around my neck, gave me a big smackeroo, and asked if I'd eaten yet.

Well this threw me completely. Talk about stealing one's thunder. There were no questions, no third degree, no interest in what I had been up to in the last twenty four hours at all. This was bloody odd. This girl was very different to anyone I had ever met.

As Whisky was hungry we went down to the restaurant and I had a second lunch. We chatted about fairly general things and returned to my room.

She seemed perturbed. I asked her what was wrong. She said she had something important to tell me but that it was probably best to wait.

I hate that, don't you? I insisted she told me what was bothering her, and so in the end, after some persuasion, she did.

What she had to tell me was important. It was important because in her mind she thought it would almost certainly make me head straight back to England on the next available flight.

She told me that she was Muslim, had been married before, and had a three year old son.

'That's wonderful!' I said. 'What's his name and what is he

like? When can I meet him?'

The look on Whisky's face was a picture. It was a look of utter joy and relief.

'His name is Keyowan. You sure you really don't mind?' she said.

'Why on earth should I mind Whisky?' I replied. 'I have two children. Does that bother you?'

'No, of course not.'

'Well then there isn't a problem, is there?' She shook her head and kissed me again.

Knowing that she already had a child was a relief. I had not yet told Whisky of the old chop, chop operation and that I was not, in that sense, a complete man. The thought had worried me for some time.

It was now easy to relate the story of my black balls and she just fell about laughing.

And so the first skeletons in the cupboard came out for both of us and were successfully laid to rest.

The next day saw us in Siam Park, a large family theme complex on the outskirts of Bangkok, quite close to the King's Palace. Whisky had brought along her little boy Keyowan to meet me. This, I instinctively knew, was going to be an important day. If I didn't get on with this little boy I was dead in the water. But he was a Thai little boy, and didn't speak any English. Fortunately he was a great kid and after his initial shyness, he just seemed to accept me.

This was a magical place for kids of any age, there was so much to do. Unfortunately as Keyowan was only just three years old he was frightened of the big rides and I had to be content with the smaller ones, all of which gave me a headache. Up and down, round and round, up and down again. Normally I hate this type of fairground attraction but I had to make a good impression, so I suffered in silence.

After about two hours of 'mind-blowing fun' I was feeling

very hot and sickly. Whisky suggested sitting down to have some lunch. Thank goodness for that I thought, because one more ride and I would definitely have been physically sick.

We sat at a table in a lovely open air theatre. On the stage there was a Thai folk band playing old standards from the sixties. As I sat and watched them with my legs crossed and my raised foot moving to the beat, Whisky told me I was being very rude. Apparently it is the height of bad manners in Thailand to point with your feet. I wasn't aware that I was actually pointing at anyone, with my feet, or anything else for that matter. However it was explained to me that because my foot was facing in the general direction of the band this in itself constituted pointing and, to make matters worse, I was moving my foot up and down which drew attention to said foot.

'Well what am I supposed to do with my feet then?' I asked.

'Keep out of way, under chair or table, more polite,' Whisky replied, shoving a very large sausage into Keyowan's very small mouth.

'Can I still move my foot in time with the music, or is that considered impolite?' I asked, 'Because for me to have to keep my feet still when there is music playing is virtually impossible!' I added.

'Fine Mike, just don't point,' said Whisky with an air of frustration at the ineptitude of her English partner.

I further learned that in Thailand the head is considered sacred and the feet are considered dirty. So one should never touch a Thai's head and should keep one's feet out of the way whenever possible.

'Can I point with my finger?' I asked, eager to not make another mistake.

'Only children and objects. You never point at adult, very impolite,' Whisky replied, continuing my education.

Keyowan then dropped a Thai coin he was playing with on to the floor and it started to roll away. I went to put my foot on it to stop it rolling, as you do.

'Mike, No!' Whisky yelled so loudly that it made me jump.

'What the hell have I done wrong now?' I asked.

'Must not put foot on King's head!' Whisky said. 'If people see you they hit you!'

'I didn't know the King was in the park,' I said sarcastically.

'Mike, don't be funny. It very bad to do. King like a God in Thailand, everyone respect very much. Must never put foot on coin or bank note, never say bad thing about King.'

Ah, I thought, very similar to the way we respect our own Royal family!

In fact the devotion all Thais show towards their King is very touching. At the Atlanta Olympics you may well have noticed the reaction of the Thai boxer who won a gold medal. The first thing he did was to get a photograph of his King and wave it above his head for all the world to see.

'I have so much to learn Whisky,' I said rather meekly.

'I know Mike, no worry, I teach you good way to do. Would you like a drink?' she asked.

'Only if I'm not going to upset anyone,' I replied.

Whisky laughed and went to get me and Keyowan a drink from the nearby cafe. We had a great day together in this park, and I distinctly remember feeling like a family. It felt right. This was where I belonged, with these two wonderful people.

Whisky looked lovely that day. She wore a pretty summer dress and her long black hair glistened in the sun. I was a happy man. For me this was when I first fell in love with her, when I knew for sure that I wanted to spend the rest of my life by her side. For her part at least on this day she learned that I would probably make a good father for her little boy, as long as I wasn't asked too often to go on things that go up, down, round and round.

We left the park around five in the afternoon and Whisky said she would like to take me to meet her grandmother as she lived fairly close by. I said I thought that would be lovely, and we boarded a bus.

Now I would for the first time, not feel so much like a tourist. It was only a short journey and as we got off the bus I could see we were in a residential area.

We walked down a street with houses on either side. Many people were milling around, children playing, men tattling with cars, women behind trellis tables cooking Thai food that smelt wonderful as you walked by. Everyone we passed smiled. The same smile I had experienced in Siam Park, a smile of approval, a seeming acceptance of us as a family unit. It felt good.

Finally we arrived outside her grandmother's house. It was small, detached, and stood on its own little plot of land with a small garden at the front.

Her grandmother came to the front door and let us in. She was about the same height as Whisky, fairly frail looking, and her face had those telling lines of experience. She had a lovely welcoming smile and I liked her straight away. She spoke a little English and so we sat and chatted happily for about an hour. The obligatory photo albums appeared and I discovered that I was not the first westerner to enter this house. Her daughter, Whisky's Mom's sister, had married an American, and was now living in Los Angeles.

We eventually said our farewells and walked back down the road to the main highway. It was now around ten o'clock at night and there were still many people about, and still the wonderful smell of food cooking. Whisky insisted we wait for a bus because it was cheaper than a taxi. We waited for ages. Lots of buses passed by but apparently none of them were going where we wanted to go. Keyowan was very tired and asleep in my arms. I finally insisted that we get a taxi and Whisky agreed.

About twenty minutes later the taxi stopped outside a shopping complex to let Whisky and Keyowan out. I offered to walk with them to their home but Whisky refused, insisting that I should continue on in the taxi back to my hotel where she would see me the following day.

'What time tomorrow?' I asked.

'Noon,' Whisky replied, and with that we parted. It had

been a wonderful day, and I felt a warm glow of contentment which unfortunately didn't last very long. I was in for another fall.

At noon the next day, no Whisky. The same at one, two and three o'clock.

I went downstairs to have something to eat. I chatted to the Indian manager of the restaurant who informed me that when someone in Bangkok said, 'See you at Noon,' it meant anytime between twelve midday and four o'clock in the afternoon, depending on the traffic. So, somewhat reassured, I continued to wait.

Six o'clock, still no Whisky. I was now really concerned. My western perceptions said that if she couldn't meet me she would have telephoned.

Unfortunately I couldn't contact her. I didn't even know her address. All my letters had been sent to The Landmark. I decided to telephone The Landmark, being my only point of contact. All I was told was, 'Miss Warune not well, sir.' I couldn't ask for any further information as I didn't want to drop her in it. She had obviously got some days off work by telling them she was ill. This probably explained the taxi floor episode. There was nothing I could do but wait. I bought another book and started to read. I then went through the longest night of my life. I couldn't sleep, I just paced the floor of my room, smoked a lot of cigarettes, and drank a lot of coffee. Funny what the old love bug can do to your system when it bites you!

The following day, feeling really lost and confused, I popped over to The Huntsman Pub for a drink. Whisky wasn't there of course and fortunately neither was anyone who knew me. I returned to my hotel at one o'clock in the afternoon, went up to my room and lay on the bed. I really thought that I had been abandoned, but for what possible reason? Perhaps her grandmother didn't like me, perhaps Keyowan didn't like me. She might even have had an accident! I felt so helpless and was very depressed. I even rang Clive in England who suggested waiting another day and then to return home if I was able to get my air ticket changed. For whatever reason it seemed pretty obvious to me now that Whisky did not wish to continue our relationship, because even if she was ill or had been involved in an accident she would surely have found a way to let me know what was going on.

At four o'clock I was lying on the bed half asleep and heard a knock on the door. I got off the bed, walked over to the door and opened it. Outside in the corridor stood Whisky, smiling broadly.

'Where the hell have you been Whisky? I've been worried sick!' I said, a little less than calmly.

'Sit down Mike. You're shaking. Are you not feeling well?' she replied, very calmly, and entered the room.

'Of course I'm bloody shaking! I've been shaking for hours! Where have you been? Why on earth didn't you telephone me?'

'Mike your face very red. Are you sure you feel all right?'

'No, I don't feel all right. What the hell have I got to feel all right about? I've been stuck in this hot and sticky hotel for twenty four hours thinking you'd ridden off into the sunset, I'm really pissed off Whisky! Why didn't you telephone me?'

'I'm sorry Mike but Keyowan really sick, couldn't leave him, no phone at home. But you shouldn't worry so much, I am okay. Chai Yen Yen.'

'Chai Yen Yen' means 'Take it easy' and let me assure you the Thais have got 'taking it easy' off to a fine art! There is a Thai philosophy that would have been very useful if I had known about it at this time. It states,

'If you go on a journey and arrive at your destination, that's fine. If you go on a journey and do not arrive at your destination, that's fine as well.'

One hell of a way to live, and it wouldn't work in the west. In Whisky's view it would only have been necessary to telephone me if she hadn't been all right. As she was all right there was obviously no need to telephone me. We argued for ages about this, and in the end I gave up as I wasn't getting anywhere at all. We had to agree to differ on what I saw as good manners versus bad manners. It was our first cultural clash, and there would be others.

We didn't have long together on this occasion because Whisky had to be at work early the following day. We had a meal together and then telephoned Karla from my room. Back in England Clive had given me some money to pass on to Karla, together with some photos and a letter. Whisky had not as yet met Karla but spoke to her on the telephone to arrange a get- together the following evening. With that accomplished we said our goodbyes and she left.

I didn't see Whisky the following day as she was at The Huntsman. After she had finished her work, we hailed a taxi and went to meet Clive's wife.

The Thai view of a person's status is not unlike the caste system of India. Clive had told me that Karla felt nervous about meeting Whisky because she, as a seamstress, felt inferior to Whisky who was a waitress. I broached the subject of status with Whisky. She told me that Thais do tend to mix only with people of their own status, but, in her opinion, it was all a bit silly really. Just as Bangkok's architecture mixed the old with the new, ideas were changing.

She was absolutely right because they got on very well indeed. I couldn't get a word in at all. I just sat and listened to the two of them chatting away happily in Thai, occasionally looking at me and giggling together. We duly passed over the items Clive had sent and in return Karla gave me a bag containing presents for my children, two dolls that she had made. This was most unexpected and very kind I thought. She was a lovely girl and as Whisky pointed out in the taxi on the way back, a very genuine lady.

The following day saw Whisky change from the day to night shift at the hotel. She came to see me in the afternoon and then went off to work at five o'clock. I asked her if it would be all right if I came over to The Huntsman later for a drink. She said that it would be fine as long as I didn't give any indication that we were an item.

Now what in the hell did she mean by that! Was she ashamed of me, or what? Why didn't she want her friends at work to know about me? Why did everything in this country have to be so 'cloak and dagger?'

An Englishman, I would meet later in my travels who lived in Bangkok, used to sum it all up with one word 'TIT' This Is Thailand, don't question it, just accept it.

8. More Wine Dear?

The Huntsman Pub, where I had originally met Whisky, was now going to be a major player in our relationship. The place that I was at first so grateful to, I would slowly come to distrust and detest. It was the place where I would spend many hours reading books, supping beer and coffee and listening to the band. It was also the place where I would meet many interesting people that would have a major impact on future events. Spending all night in a pub is not something I had in the past often done. I'm not a big drinker and have found such activity, or more to the point lack of activity, boring. But I felt it was important that Whisky knew where I was, or again more to the point where I wasn't. This was Bangkok and the temptations were everywhere.

There were only a few days left before I would be returning to England and very little time to spend with Whisky as she was now back at work.

I wanted to be in a microcosm of our own where I could tell her my innermost feelings and preferably with a romantic backdrop to complete my fantasy.

Fortunately the opportunity effortlessly presented itself. While I was sitting in The Huntsman, reading yet another James Herriot classic, Whisky informed me that the next day was her day off. She had been able to swap with one of the other girls to give us a little more time to spend with each other. I suggested we go somewhere special for a meal as it would be our last opportunity to be together for some time. She agreed and we arranged to meet the following evening at six o'clock.

Sitting there hour after hour in The Huntsman, watching what went on around me, enabled me to see just what I was up against. The majority of the customers were western business men, fairly affluent western business men. As Whisky was one of the most attractive waitresses in there she was constantly being chatted up. It was like being a fly on the wall. She had to be pleasant to everyone, no matter how unpleasant or suggestive they were to her. Sitting there would become sheer bloody torture. It was a high class establishment. The Landmark was one of the top ten hotels in Bangkok. But that fact wasn't very reassuring to me realising that the vast majority of the customers in the place could probably buy and sell me ten times over, or at least their company expense budgets enabled them to be a lot more 'flash with the cash.'

So there they all were, staring me in the face, my rivals. It gave me an incredibly insecure feeling I can tell you. Why on earth was she bothering with me? It looked like she had the pick of the male western world parading in front of her every night. I felt that at any moment, what I desired most could be snatched away in front of my eyes. It was not to be endured.

Back in my hotel room that night I made a decision. I was going to ask Whisky to marry me. I was fairly sure she would not say yes, but I hoped she would at least not say no. I was going back to England in forty eight hours and needed some indication of her feelings towards me. I could not justify to my family and friends another trip to Thailand without a solid reason for returning.

I could feel the warmth in her smile. I could sense a true depth of feeling when we kissed. If this were a local girl in England I would know instinctively where I stood. But Whisky was Thai and not like anyone I had ever met before. Doubts swirled around my head. My senses were confused. Would she feel pressurised and completely back off? I would be opening Pandora's box and firmly grabbing it's only contents - hope. What a dinner date this was going to be!

The restaurant chosen was French, and very high class. The Thai waiters bowed so low I feared they would suffer back pains in later life.

We had a delightful meal accompanied by a bottle of Mateus Rose chosen by Whisky from the wine list. The waiters were so attentive that an opportunity just didn't arise for me to pronounce my undying love. I tried several times but every time one of the waiters would pop up bowing and scraping around the table. I think they must have known. They didn't get a tip! Oh all right they did, but it was all very frustrating.

As we left the restaurant Whisky fell over. I thought she had tripped. I picked her up and asked if she was hurt.

'No, I do not think so,' she said. 'But my head go round and round.'

'You're drunk!' I said laughing. 'Why didn't you tell me drink affected you like this?' She had only had one glass.

'I never have wine before,' she said. 'Only Coke, tea and coffee, but mostly just water.'

It then suddenly occurred to me, Muslims don't drink. Oh dear! I've really blown it in a big way now. I've made her sin in the eyes of her God. She'll never forgive me. I hailed a taxi and helped her in. She seemed to be asleep, eyes closed and a silly grin on her face.

'Come on Whisky, wake up.' Her eyes opened. 'Ah, signs of life. Can you tell the driver where your house is and this time I insist on making sure you arrive at your door safely. You're in a right state and I feel utterly responsible. Now it's no good you arguing I really do insist. It's the least I can do. I had no idea that one glass of wine would.............'

'Do shut up Mike, I have bad headaish. Can we go back to your hotel, would you mind?'

Mind, would I mind? Gadzooks, the Gods were suddenly with me. She told the driver where to go, put her head on my shoulder, and closed her eyes again. I kissed her forehead and said,

'I love you Whisky.' A little faint wobbly voice replied,

'I love you too Mike.' I knew I would be returning to Bangkok.

She stayed with me that night. I undressed her and put her into the big double bed. I sat on the edge of the bed, and just looked at my little Thai lady for ages. Her body was so beautiful, so perfectly formed, and unfortunately so soundly asleep. I eventually undressed and slid in beside her. As our naked bodies touched she put her arms around me, and tears uncontrollably trickled down my face. They were tears of absolute joy and contentment. Everything was all right with the world, and I fell to sleep.

The next morning however was a bit different. She was sober, awake, and very playful. It was like being a teenager again on a voyage of discovery. She took one look at my now fully functional and very eager to get started tackle and said, 'Oh Mike. Why so big?'

Now please be assured here that a male stud I am not. I have it on good authority that western men on the whole are larger than eastern men, and that is what must have prompted this comment. But also let me assure you that boosted with confidence it grew by at least one more inch. I was ready. Oh boy was I ready!

It was unforgettable, unsurpassable. The soft circles of her touch wafted around my body like satin shimmering in a sea breeze. Snake like she coiled and slithered and I melted into her with a closeness I have never known. Her finger tip touches titillated and taunted my every nerve ending until I tingled and lingered over every oral delight and she purred and stretched and arched her body in a rainbow of delectation. I had never known of such intimacy. It was all consuming, teasing and tantalising. Her soft sounds whispered in appreciation and they wafted through my senses as gentle as the desert sands trickling between ones toes. We slid into dreamlessness.

So I then asked her to marry me, she said yes, and we lived happily ever after.

Now you don't believe that for one minute do you? My life couldn't possibly be that simple could it? There was still a long, long way to go but unofficially engaged we were and my life now had direction.

9. If You Hear Someone Cry

We had a wonderful last day together. After a morning spent in bed we went for a walk in Queen's Park. We were just like a couple of kids, we even played on the swings. We then went shopping so that I could buy a couple of shirts.

Thai silk shirts are not only excellent but also very inexpensive. I had earlier discovered that Whisky was not exactly over endowed with clothes. Taking care of herself and her son left little money to buy anything else. I was amazed when she told me, for instance, that she only had one dress, the pretty one she wore at Siam Park.

'Why are you so shocked Mike? I can only wear one at a time,' she laughed.

I tried several times to buy her a new dress until she said, quite sharply,

'Why you keep wanting to buy me something Mike? I don't need anything!'

Oh joy and bliss abounding. There was one woman in this entire world who didn't need anything, and she was standing next to me! I had won the lottery, months before it even started. God had obviously decided I had now paid for all my past transgressions and had nipped off to pick on someone else. Poor bastard!

I suppose realistically I have a very romantic view of a loving relationship. I have always had a picture in my mind of how it should be. The best songs I have ever written have been love songs. Back in England, a few days later, I would write another song for Whisky, with words this time, that very simply summed this up.

"Long before I met you, I knew you well,
You were always there in my mind."

Not the greatest love lyric in the world maybe, but that was how I truly felt. Many girls I had known, I had been married and produced two wonderful children but never before had I been involved in any relationship that came close to the picture I had in my mind. The picture that had now become a reality with this beautiful little Thai lady.

Her technique for buying clothes for me was excellent. We would walk through many shops and I would point out which shirts I liked best. I would then go for a drink while Whisky returned to said shops and bought the required shirts. In this way I paid a lot less than I would have done shopping on my own. There are, I learnt, two prices available.

1. Thai trader to Thai customer - low price.

2. Thai trader to Thai customer with western guy in tow - as much as they can get out of your wallet.

At four o'clock that afternoon Whisky had to go to work, so we said our emotional goodbyes in my hotel room. She promised she would write and promised she would wait for me. She reconfirmed that she wanted to be with me, and I knew that she was telling me the truth. I told her there was now much we had to find out about with regard to Visas as we didn't want to be in the same position as Clive and Karla if it could be avoided. I assured her that I would return to Bangkok as soon as I was able so that we could approach the British Embassy.

Whisky didn't say a lot. She didn't seem over interested in this conversation about Visas. She just said that she would miss me very much and hoped I would return soon.

My primary purpose at this point in time was to get the wheels in motion so that I was able to marry Whisky and take her to England.

That last evening sitting in The Huntsman Pub, waiting for the painful moment when I would have to leave for the airport, was not pleasant. There was one particular customer who was being very attentive to Whisky. I wanted to hit him. Well the least I wanted to do was to tell him to back off. Ridiculous really, looking back, just how possessive and jealous I was on many occasions in that pub. I'm not normally the possessive type but this was different, this was Bangkok. I was leaving and that far too good looking customer was staying.

Something else became apparent during the two hours I sat there. At least two of the other waitresses knew about our relationship. They would, many times, look over to the table where I was sitting and smile or giggle.

This however made me feel more secure. It was a form of acceptance. Perhaps the 'cloak and dagger' stuff was now behind us.

Finally the dreaded hour arrived and I asked Whisky for the bill. She brought it over and slipped a white beer mat into my hand.

On the reverse was written,

Please come back again
if you don't comback
I will died.
If you hear someone cry,
looking at me first.

'I'm fillin' up Tommy.'

I wanted to hold her, but couldn't. I looked into her eyes, mouthed, 'I love you,' walked to the pub exit and out into the arcade. Whisky had followed me into the arcade, and so had three of the other waitresses who all gave me a lovely Wai. I returned the Wai, looked longingly at Whisky and started to walk through the arcade. She, very surprisingly, walked with me, saying nothing. We reached the foot of the steep flight of stairs that led up to the Sukhumvit Road. Whisky let me kiss her on the cheek as no one was around to see. She said,

'Please come back Mike. I will miss you so much.'

I assured her again that I would return and set off up the steep flight of stone steps. At the top I turned, not really expecting Whisky to still be there, but she was. I smiled and waved. She then, very slowly, put her hands together and bowed in the most gracious Wai I had ever seen. It was the first Wai I had received from Whisky and therefore all the more effective. All the way back to the hotel the tears just came trickling down my face, it was a very emotional experience for me. No woman had ever shown me this much respect. It's funny though what occurs to you at times. I thought to myself that if this was a musical, this scene needed an epic song. Something along the lines of 'Unchained Melody' or a Whitney Houston classic.

Two hours later, back on the big metal bird, I was drinking whisky again, heading in the wrong bloody direction, and writing a love song on the back of a fag packet.

10. Failure Seemed Inevitable

On the first evening back in England Wilf popped round. I had asked him to come over as I wanted him to sing the song that I had written for Whisky. Write songs I can, sing them I can't.

I was fairly sure he would be his usual self, honest and critical. But this time he wasn't. Not critical anyway. He listened to the story of my trip very attentively and when I had finished he said,

'That's beautiful Mick, really beautiful. I'm fillin' up 'ere our kid.'

I think it was the bit about the Wai at the end that really got to him. He was also able to see, from the many photos I now had of Whisky, that she was a very beautiful lady. He looked at one of the photos for what seemed like ages, lit a cigarette, and then looked at me in a way that only Wilf can look.

'I hope this works out for you Mick. I've known you longer than Whisky has been alive, and that's a long time. I know you better than anyone. I've seen you up and I've seen you down, but I've never seen you glow before. I hope to God nothing goes wrong because you'll never get over it, never.'

A silence hung in the air.

He then stubbed out the cigarette, rose from his chair and adjusted the microphone stand.

'Okay then Mick let's have a listen to this song then. I presume you want it deep and meaningful. Crack open a bottle of throat lubricant, I'll need to be pissed.'

It was going to be a good night.

The next morning, sober, I played the tape we had recorded and it sounded nearly as good as the night before, which is always the acid test. I penned a quick letter to Whisky, and posted it together with the tape.

At around this time I had a big row with my mother. I went to see her to show her the photographs I had taken of Whisky in

Thailand, and to tell her what I thought my future held in store. Sadly she just didn't want to know. She kept referring to what our brave boys went through in the second world war.

'What the hell has any of that got to do with Whisky,' I asked in vain.

I tried and tried to counter this prejudice, but it was deep rooted and somehow she seemed to link Thailand and Japan together as responsible. I was amazed how anyone, let alone my mother, could hold such feelings about an individual that was born twenty three years after the events she was referring to. This angered me very much and in the end I said some very harsh things to her that I regretted the moment I walked out of her flat. Having said that I still believe her attitude at the time was unfeeling, unnecessary and very hurtful. We did not see each other to speak to again for over a year.

Over the next few weeks I was very busy. There was much to find out regarding the immigration laws and all things pertaining to settlement of a Thai national in this country.

I would have to prove that I was a reliable sponsor, that I could support Whisky, and eventually her little boy, financially.

None of this I foresaw as a problem. I had always kept my affairs in order and had a good income from my business. But just in case I needed some back-up, I asked several friends and colleagues to write references for me.

My bank manager, my accountant, my building society and any friends I could stitch up to write nice things about me. All this was very simple and straightforward.

The most worrying thing was this so called Primary Purpose Law. Clive had put me in touch with the lady he used to translate Karla's letters. She was Thai, and married to an Englishman. She was most helpful and informed me that out of the last fifty or so cases she had heard of where English guys were trying to get a Thai lady into England, all had failed. The one thing that the majority of these cases did have in common was the fact that the couples had met via an agency.

At this time Clive was waiting for the documentation to arrive from the British Embassy in Bangkok stating in writing the reasons for the refusal of their visa application, and a transcription of their interviews. This would be valuable information for me and Clive promised to send a copy as soon as it arrived.

Geraint, my friend and accountant, told me about a client of his that had a friend who was engaged to a Thai lady. He had for some time apparently been trying to get her into England. He gave me the telephone number of this gentleman, and I rang him the very next day.

He sounded a bit of a rough diamond but seemed friendly and very willing to talk to me. He had a very strong black country accent and from my conversation on the telephone I had a fair picture of him in my mind. I thought he would be a bit rough looking, probably an ex- fifties Rock and Roller. He probably wasn't very well off financially, could well be on the dole. He definitely would live in a council house, smoke, and have strong views about the state of the nation.

Well I was close! He was actually a millionaire, lived in a massive converted barn complex out in the country, and on his own. As I drove up the very long and winding private drive, I spotted a Rolls Royce Corniche outside the house, just to the left of the large ornamental pond. As I drew up beside the very ornate oak front door he appeared from behind it.

'Allo our kid. Found the place all right then. Come on in and 'ave a drink?'

He showed me into a very large and spacious lounge. Everything around me looked expensive and I couldn't see an ashtray. He didn't smoke, I hadn't even got that right. He did however have strong views on the state of the nation. Specifically the state of the nation's view about Englishmen marrying foreign ladies, and in particular he wasn't too keen on the British Embassy in Bangkok.

'They're bastards in that Embassy Mick, real bastards!' he sounded like Wilf.

'Do yow know what they said to me Mick, them bastards at that Embassy?'

'I dread to think my friend.' I said.

'They said they wouldn't give me a visa for my fiancé to come to England because I ain't got proper sewerage facilities.'

'Really?' I said. 'How extraordinary!'

'I ain't on mains sewerage, see Mick, I've got one of them sceptic tanks.'

'Oh I see,' I said, although I didn't.

'I showed 'em diagrams, plans, and ev'ryfin Mick, but they didn't wanna know.'

'Oh dear,' I sympathised unsuccessfully.

'And do you know what I told 'em Mick? Them bastards at that Embassy!'

I shook my head in fearful anticipation.

'I told 'em my sceptic tank was full of shit, like their effin' Embassy!'

'Oh, well done!' I said supportively. 'I expect they were impressed with your sense of humour.'

'Sense of 'umour Mick, they ain't got no sense of 'umour.'

We talked for some time and I found his experience very useful. He showed me a lot of documentation of transcribed interviews held at the Embassy between Thai ladies and the British Embassy staff. Fascinating stuff to be sure, and quite frightening to think Whisky would have to go through a similar ordeal. He suggested going to see a lawyer he knew in London who specialised in immigration law.

'Yow'll need all the 'elp yow can get Mick. It's an effin' minefield.'

The next day, after making sure my toilet was flushing properly, I phoned the London lawyer and made an appointment for the following week.

What I remember most about my first ever visit to a London lawyer and made an appointment for the following week.

What I remember most about my first ever visit to a London lawyer was that he had a bad cold and kept sneezing.

Other than that he did a damn good job of convincing me that he could present our case for a Visa in such a way that success was virtually guaranteed. It would of course cost a lot of money for him to do this, about five thousand pounds as I remember. In addition it would probably involve him accompanying me to Bangkok to tutor Whisky for the interview at the Embassy.

I listened carefully to everything he said which took about two hours. I thanked him for his time, hoped his cold would get better, and said I would be in touch after giving it all some thought.

On the train heading back to Birmingham International, eating a cheese and tomato sandwich, I was greatly perturbed. I had seen a man, an international lawyer, who had advised me to spend five thousand pounds, plus a trip to Bangkok, to prepare a case for the Embassy to judge the genuineness of our relationship. He had even advocated lying where he deemed it was necessary. Why, I thought, is the truth not good enough? At least the truth won't cost five thousand pounds to prepare.

I made a decision. We would have to approach the Embassy with the truth, the whole truth, and nothing but the truth. It was all we could afford!

So having just saved myself five thousand pounds I went to the buffet car and treated myself to a cream cake, as a sweet, to follow my cheese and tomato main course.

I hoped the truth would be good enough but feared that it would not. I had learned of many more failures than successes. The statement made to Clive and Karla by an Embassy official kept coming to the front of my mind. 'But Mr. and Mrs. Richards, we are not stopping you being together, we are only stopping you being together in England!'

The situation was frightening. I now fully realised how much power the British Embassy had to make or break our future happiness.

A thought occurred to me at this time. It was something that I had learned from a Japanese Professor of music. He used to say, 'Look through the eyes of the child. How is the child perceiving what you are trying to teach?'

So I tried to think as a British Embassy Immigration Official. What criteria had they to work from? What were they looking for? What reasons would they have to fail us?

The first step would be to find out exactly why they had failed Clive and Karla, I desperately needed the transcript of their interview. When I finally received this, several weeks later, one thing was abundantly clear to me. If I had been the interviewing officer, looking at the facts presented to me, I would probably have failed their application.

I now knew Clive very well. Since my return to England we had talked many times on the telephone. I felt very sorry for him and the situation he was in. But I had to look at this whole Visa thing logically and unemotionally if I was to understand the standpoint of the British Embassy.

The documentation stated that Clive and Karla had met and got engaged within a couple of days of meeting each other. Clive had then returned to England and they had written many letters to each other. He subsequently returned to Thailand where they got married and applied for a Visa. At the time they got married they had probably only spent, in total, a few days together, two people who did not speak the same language and from two entirely different cultures. They had devised a simple story of how they met, on the advice of Fagin, to cover the fact that they were actually introduced by an agency. The story was unlikely. The relationship was very short and Karla did not speak any English. These were the facts presented to the Embassy.

I rang the Thai Embassy in London and had a very informative chat with a very helpful Thai lady. She told me that a lot of marriages between Thai ladies and western men often end badly, leaving the girl alone and frightened in the foreign country. The Thai Embassy would then often have to help these girls by paying for a plane ticket back to Thailand. She was very supportive of my request for information and recommended that we take great care with our relationship. Mainly she suggested to give ourselves enough time to be sure that we wanted to be together for the right reasons. Good advice to be sure.

It was now very apparent to me that rushing off to the British Embassy to ask for a Visa was likely to end in failure.

My deliberations had convinced me of several things :-
The British Embassy in Bangkok obviously has a very difficult job to do in assessing genuine requests for settlement in England.

It would be extremely naive to believe that falling in love with Whisky in itself gave me the right to expect England to welcome her with open arms.

The Embassy have understandable difficulty granting a Visa to a Thai girl who doesn't speak English, and who has only known a western man for a matter of days.

So we needed to present a strong case. As Whisky already spoke English very well longevity of the relationship seemed to be the major factor.

More time would mean more trips to Thailand. More trips would cost a lot of money. Problem!

11. Traumatic Times

The telephone can be one's best friend or one's worst enemy.

I was now telephoning Bangkok at least three times a week, and it's very expensive. But what's money got to do with it when you're talking to the one you love? Quite a lot actually. My resources were now at an all time low. I didn't know how the hell I was going to pay the massive telephone bill, let alone get back to Bangkok.

Right on cue an offer popped through my letter box.

'Have a Barclaycard,' it said.

'Yes,' I replied. 'Thank you very much!'

My credit rating was good and I ended up with several brightly coloured credit cards from these wonderfully helpful people.

'You're just diggin' yourself a pit Mick.'

'I know Wilf, but what's the alternative?'

'Celibacy Mick.'

'Exactly Wilf.'

And so love on an overdraft it was going to have to be for a while.

Talking to Whisky on the telephone was both elating and depressing. The British Telecom advertisement, 'It's good to talk' is true when what is being said on the other end of the line is what you want to hear. Sometimes Whisky sounded cool and unresponsive. It was often just because she was tired. But one's mind doesn't always accept that as a reason. When the telephone was replaced and the call was over I would analyse every sentence. A bit silly maybe, but that's what I did.

Invariably I would then telephone Clive to discuss my feelings. He would do the same if something was bothering him. We became very good friends swapping insecurities.

One weekend was particularly memorable. I had gone to Wrexham to stay with Clive and on the Saturday morning a translation of Karla's latest letter arrived through the letter box. It started something like this:

Good news darling, the village have asked us to
provide a Bell for the Temple.

Karla being a Buddhist took her religion very seriously. She once said to Clive that she hoped this life would be her last attempt at getting it right so that she could go to nirvana, or heaven as we call it in the west. She maintained that she had lived forty eight lives before this one and was now very tired. Part of this religion is concerned with 'making merit' This means doing good deeds such as giving to the poor or the temple. Apparently this giving helps one to get to nirvana and, in simple terms, this was what Karla believed.

Now Clive's finances were worse than mine.

'What the hell's this all about? It's making merit again isn't it?' said Clive, very perturbed.

His face was a picture. He kept looking at the letter in disbelief.

'How much is a bell going to cost?' he asked me.

'I don't know Clive. How big are we talking here?' I asked. 'The liberty bell's quite impressive but the one hanging over my fireplace would be a lot cheaper. Basically Clive we're talking brass here.'

'You mean it's going to cost a lot?' he looked really worried now.

'No Clive, I mean they are made of brass,' I replied smiling.

'Well how much is brass?' he asked, not smiling.

'We're back to size again Clive, and then there's the cost of forging it. I shouldn't think it will be cheap, even in Bangkok,' I replied, trying to sound knowledgeable.

'Oh good grief! I needed this like I need a hole in the head Mike.'

'A hole in the head would be easier and a lot less expensive Clive.'

We both laughed and went down the pub. Above the bar was a big brass bell. Buddha must definitely have a sense of humour, I thought.

That afternoon we visited Chester to buy presents for our respective ladies.

We had now definitely decided to return to Bangkok together. Martin would also be there at the same time with Gow, so it would be a bit of a reunion.

I left Clive the following day, still worried about the cost of a bell, and returned home.

A few days later I spoke to Whisky on the telephone. She sounded different. There was something in her voice that sounded noticeably different, and it definitely wasn't just tiredness. It's ever so difficult to explain what I mean by different but I knew instinctively that something was wrong, but what? She wouldn't tell me. She just said she was tired and that she wasn't feeling too well, but I knew this wasn't the whole story. Something had drastically changed. I had to ask her if she loved me to get a response to that effect, and even though she confirmed that she did, it didn't sound at all convincing. You just know, don't you! It's in the tone of voice. I must have driven Clive mad discussing it on the telephone, but I was very worried.

The last four weeks leading up to returning to Bangkok were traumatic for me. I wanted to know what was wrong. I needed to know what was wrong. I had opened my heart to friends and family about Whisky and I would feel a complete and utter fool if she, as I thought she might, finished our relationship.

This concern also made me realise that actually I still knew very little about her. I came up with a hundred reasons for her change in attitude but I wasn't even close. Then I didn't understand Thailand, the land of a thousand smiles. I didn't understand Bangkok, the city of Angels. I would, in time, learn that each smile means something different and that it was very hard to find an angel in Bangkok.

12. The Trio Returns

This time it was an even cheaper air fare but meant travelling to Clive's house in my car and flying together from Manchester airport. I arrived at Clive's the night before we were due to travel. After we had eaten I rang Whisky at the Huntsman, and then wished I hadn't. I had hoped she would sound excited that I was on my way, but not so. She was still unresponsive and cool. She even sounded a little annoyed that I had phoned, or that could have been my imagination working overtime. I slept little that night wondering what I had to face the next day in Bangkok.

Travelling with this middle eastern airline included a stop over of four hours in Dubai and also meant no booze on the journey. So no whisky on route. In fact no Whisky when we arrived at Bangkok airport. Where was she? Karla was there to meet Clive with her family, friends, and flowers but she had seen nothing of Whisky. I knew it, my worst fears were confirmed. I walked up and down the airport several times trying to spot her in the crowds of people milling around. No luck! She just wasn't there, so I returned to Clive and Karla and suggested we all get a taxi to the hotel.

There was an emptiness in my stomach, a void where my heart should be. I had travelled seven thousand miles in anticipation of seeing Whisky. I had re-run the scene in my mind and savoured it in my dreams. I had envisaged a face in the crowd aglow with love on catching sight of me, the rush into each other's arms as we both strove through the crowds in the reception area. But in the sea of faces was not the one face I longed to see. I was distraught. I was lost. I was totally and irretrievably shattered.

I carried my case and my misery towards the taxi rank. Then she appeared.
'I'm sorry, sorry, sorry, traffic, traffic!' she let out breathlessly.

My relief was intense. I suppressed my feelings of a moment before down into the depths of my soul. She was here. That was all that mattered.

The taxi headed to our hotel. We held hands and we chatted, but there was a tension in her. I could feel it. Someone had built a brick wall, but who and why?

Family problems is what she said but I just knew instinctively there was more. She would talk to me about it later, she said, and for the moment, I had to be content.

In the hotel reception we met up with Martin and Gow and drank coffee while we exchanged experiences. Martin, having been in Saudi Arabia, looked disgustingly tanned and healthy. He was back in Bangkok to get to know Gow better. Both Clive and I gave presents to our respective ladies. To Whisky I gave a watch. She looked at it, thanked me and put it into her bag. Clive also gave a watch to Karla who reacted in an entirely different and noticeable way. She exploded into joy. It was then that I really knew something was wrong, for Whisky had always been so appreciative of the smallest kindness I had shown her.

Eventually the little reunion party split up and we all retired to our various rooms.

Whisky did not have long before she had to go to work but the good news was that she would stay with me, at the hotel, for the length of my stay in Bangkok. This was excellent. We would really have time to talk and decide what we were going to do in the future. I had much to tell her about the people I had met and all the information I had collected.

She was a little more relaxed now and promised we would have a long talk when she returned from work. I said that I would see her later in The Huntsman Pub where the rest of us were going later that night for a celebration drink. She smiled in approval, kissed me and left to go to work. It was a nice kiss, given with obvious feeling and I now thought I might be overreacting to her change in manner. Perhaps it was just family problems as she had said.

The Huntsman was busy that night but we all managed to sit at the same table. The band were amazing, all Filipino and all excellent musicians. The five piece ensemble comprised of two very attractive girl singers and guys on keyboards, bass and drums. They did mostly cover versions of up- to-date western pop music and they did it very well.

About halfway through the evening Martin suggested I ask Whisky to dance with me. I told him that I did not think this such a good idea as she was at work and the management might not like it. But he didn't give in. He called Whisky over to our table and insisted that she dance with me. Surprisingly she agreed and I followed her onto the dance floor. As we started to dance the other waitresses cheered us on. Whisky looked really embarrassed but luckily the song was half over when we hit the dance floor, so finished fairly quickly.

All the waitresses, Whisky's friends, were so nice to me, but little did I know what was going on behind my back. They were to put our relationship under a strain it didn't deserve. It was part of the reason for the change in Whisky. Slowly it became clear that these girls were constantly laying down the poison, probably out of jealousy. Not jealousy because they wanted me but jealousy of the general fact that Whisky had a western boyfriend. Many of them worked in this hotel because it brought them into contact with well-to-do western men.

The first example of this came in the form of a question Whisky asked me that same night. I had returned to my hotel with the others at about midnight. Whisky arrived about two thirty, after she had finished work. As she entered our room I could see from the look on her face that she was very concerned about something. She sat on the edge of the bed and very seriously asked me the following question,

'Mike, if I go England with you will I be maid?'

I was stunned to say the least.

'Why on earth should you ask me such a thing Whisky?'

'So why my friends keep on saying bad things happen if I marry you?' she asked in tears.

This was tricky one to handle. I did not want to appear to Whisky to be critical of her friends, whatever I thought privately I had to tread on rice paper - with care.

'They are probably concerned about you Whisky. They don't know me like you do. To them I am just another western punter here for a good time. I'll just have to prove otherwise won't I? But I don't really care what anyone else thinks. It's what you think and believe that's important.'

She calmed down, stopped crying, and we just held each other in silence for what seemed like ages.

This trip would be full of occurrences like this one. Whisky would leave me to go to work a happy lady. She would return with questions, doubts, and insecurities.

One other such example had a somewhat humorous side to it.

Whisky finally let me buy her something. She had always wanted to learn the guitar. She had received a few lessons in the past as a child at school, but then had to stop because of lack of funds. So I offered to buy a guitar and teach her. She accepted and we spent many happy hours in our hotel room playing this guitar and singing. I think the modern phrase for it is, 'Quality time together.'

One night again after work, following this purchase of a guitar, she walked into our room in tears. The so- called friends had been on at her again, and I quote :-

'What's he bought you then, this wonderful Englishman?'

'He's bought me a guitar and giving me lessons,' replied Whisky.

'Oh he's bought you a guitar, not a house or a car, but a guitar. That's going to give you a lot of security. You'll be able to busk on the Sukhumvit when he goes back to England!'

Though ludicrous, this made me burst out laughing. It was so pathetic! Where did these girls get off? Whisky was obviously upset but I tried to make her look at the whole thing with a sense of humour.

'Well your answer to that could be, 'Well at least I've got a guitar. What have you got?'

It still amazes me to this day how nice they all were to my face, sickeningly so.

I had grown to respect Whisky as a kind, intelligent, mature lady who coped with her very difficult life brilliantly well. She worked extremely hard to keep herself and her family and didn't deserve this onslaught from her friends. I offered to have a word with them but Whisky wouldn't let me. She said it would only make the situation worse.

I was beginning to understand some of the reasons for Whisky's change in attitude. During my long absences, the poisoned chatter of her so called friends had undoubtedly affected her thinking. And there was more. No wonder she was confused. Slowly now more things began to emerge about her family.

I knew that her mother and father did not live together but had not thought it wise to delve too much into this, thinking that Whisky would tell me more when she deemed the time was right.

She started to tell me a little about her father one night after work. On this particular night I was ill in bed with flu. I blame the water festival.

At this time of year everyone in Thailand throws water over each other. Not just for an hour, not just for a day, but for a whole week. It's good fun at first, especially in that heat. For me the novelty wore off after one day of being drenched to the skin, but it was probably this constant drenching that caused me to be ill.

Now it has to be said that like most men I don't suffer well. If I'm ill, everybody has to participate. It seems only fair. So there I was lying in my pit of pain when Whisky returned from work.

She looked at me, said hello and went into the bathroom. There was no, 'How are you feeling Mike?' or, 'Are you feeling better now darling?' She just went straight into the bathroom. She was in there for ages. At first I thought she was probably desperate for the loo, but after half an hour of waiting I was feeling very neglected. I did a few well rehearsed groans to encourage her to my bedside but to no avail. I waited and waited, but she stayed in the bathroom. After about an hour I finally gave in and knocked on the bathroom door. Whisky unlocked it and I saw to my amazement that she was washing her clothes. It was nearly four o'clock in the morning! I was dying a death, and she was washing her smalls!

'What are you doing? It's four o'clock in the morning. I'm ill, sweating like a pig, and you don't seem to give a damn!'

I returned to my bed, fairly content that I'd made my point here, with a fair degree of subtlety I thought.

Whisky came to the foot of the bed and gave me a look that I can only describe as daunting. The look said, 'You poor pathetic little boy.'

She then went back into the bathroom and emerged a few moments later with a wet flannel. She pulled back the bedclothes and patted the wet flannel all over my body, with such delicacy, it was very touching. She then gave me one of those daunting looks again and we both laughed.

'You're very good at that,' I said.

'I always do it for my father when he's ill,' she replied.

'Lucky man, your Dad.'

'But of course,' she replied smiling.

'Tell me a bit more about your father then,' I requested, taking full advantage of the opening.

She told me that her father was a Muslim, a strict Muslim, and that there was no way that he would ever be able to accept his daughter marrying a Christian.

'That's it then,' I said, 'back to the drawing board. I wonder what Russian women are like?' She laughed and nearly fell off the bed.

'It not that bad Mike,' she said. 'It just sad because I know he really like you if got to know you which he won't because you Christian.'

'I nearly followed that,' I said. 'So where does your father live?' I asked.

'At home,' she replied.

'Your home?' I asked puzzled.

'Yes, he have bad back so he look after my son while I go to work.'

No wonder she only had one dress. She was keeping her father as well.

'Will this make things difficult for us Whisky?' I asked with my fingers crossed.

'Not really, just sad make me, we have to take care he not find out. Mom know all about you and has read all your letters. She okay, but Dad must not know, he never accept it.'

The solicitor's boyfriend with the shotgun suddenly came to mind. But this was Bangkok, so it would probably be a hatchet. I think this was about the time I started to lock and bolt the bedroom door. I also wasn't sure if I should be pleased or not that Whisky's Mom had read all my letters. Anyway she wouldn't be drawn any further on the subject of her father. She had told me as much as she was going to tell me, and that was that! It was now obvious to me that Whisky was letting me in on things in a 'need to know' basis. No amount of coaxing or digging would extract any more information than she was prepared to give.

So my mother back in England couldn't get over her second world war prejudice, and Whisky's father was a Muslim who couldn't accept Christians. It was all going pretty well I thought!

About this time I met Jim Arthur. I was sitting on my own in The Huntsman, listening to the band as usual, when I overheard bits of a conversation going on at the table directly behind me. I turned slightly so that I was better able to see the people who were talking. There were two western guys sat opposite each other. I continued to listen. The one man's accent I recognised as from southern England somewhere. He was doing most of the talking. I realised fairly quickly from what he was saying that he lived somewhere in Bangkok. It also became plain that he was a regular visitor to The Huntsman Pub because he knew most of the waitresses by name.

I waited for a break in their conversation and introduced myself. This was a bit cheeky really as I left them with no polite alternative than to ask me to join them. But as my grandmother used to say, 'There's nought for the dumb Michael my boy!' so join them I did.

I asked Jim if he knew Whisky and he confirmed that he did. I then told him that we were seeing each other and that was my reason for being in Bangkok.

He called Whisky over. 'Why didn't you tell me you had an English boyfriend?'

Her face grew angry. I realised that this was a subject I shouldn't have mentioned but the damage had been done.

'You're a very lucky man Mike, she's a lovely, lovely girl,' said Jim kindly.

Jim was great. He had lived in Bangkok for about ten years, was married to a Thai lady called Tor and owned a small hotel called Thai House. His knowledge in regard to Thailand, the Thais, and the British Embassy was invaluable.

Back at the hotel that night I got an ear-bending off Whisky who was not at all pleased I had been talking to Jim.

Here we go again, more fodder for that part of the brain reserved for insecurities, back into the 'cloak and dagger' country.

'What's the problem?' I asked. 'Why do I have to be such a big secret?'

'Mr. Jim is customer. Customer must not know about boyfriend,' she replied.

It suddenly became clearer. The waitresses in The Huntsman relied on tips to boost their salary. Tips came mostly from men who had to be encouraged to return. All the girls, whether they were married, engaged, or courting never divulged this to customers. As far as the customers were concerned they were all free to be chatted up. This didn't mean they went off with customers, they just teased for tips. And it paid off. I believe that the hotel itself had a very strict rule about staff fraternising with guests but there again the hotel did not pay very high wages. My learning curve continued.

13. Are married or Aren't We

'You've got to go and see the bar girls Mike, it's part of the culture here.'

Clive was quite amazed that this was my third trip to Bangkok and I hadn't yet been into one of the girly bars.

Clive wasn't the only one that thought I was odd. Whisky did as well.

She believed that all men went with bar girls. It was something that all Thai women learned to accept about the majority of Thai men. Why then should foreign men be any different? It is a major industry in Thailand. Men from all over the world come to Bangkok to access the bar girls. It took ages for me to convince Whisky that all men are not like that. In England I have given up arguing with certain people who assume that because one has been to Bangkok one has partaken of the flesh in a big way. It is such a shame that this is their reaction as Bangkok has so much more to offer, and so many far better things to be famous for.

However, as I had already started to think about writing a book I thought it would be advantageous to go and have a look, just for research purposes of course. First of all, I asked Whisky if she minded me going with Clive and she said she thought it was a good idea as I should be more aware of what goes on in Bangkok.

'Soi Cowboy' was in the heart of the red light area and was quite unlike what I had expected. This was a street full of bars, one after the other and on both sides. Bright lights danced over the heads of the milling tourists. Clive led the way into one of the bars. It was wall to ceiling mirrors. Looking up I noticed, to my horror, that I was going a bit thin on top. In the middle of the floor there was a disco area with it's dancing pulsating lights. Stainless steel poles went from floor to ceiling and gyrating around them were girls - very beautiful girls - and very naked. There was about them an air of artificial gaiety. I couldn't tell whether they were happy in their work or whether the smiles were part of the act. Some looked hardened performers while others looked very innocent and so young. For the price of a Big Mac with chips they were yours!

Somehow though I didn't feel pressurised or threatened. These were experts. Everyone was there for a good time.

One young lady came over to me and offered her services. I asked how much and she said five hundred baht, which is about twelve pounds.

I asked her if she would accept two hundred and fifty baht as I wasn't very good! I don't think she appreciated the humour and walked away to another punter.

'Well. What do you think then,' Clive asked.

'I think she's lovely, very attractive and extremely sexy. They're all lovely, and they all look so happy,' I replied.

'She is a he!' Clive said, smiling broadly.

'You've gotta be joking!' I replied, seriously shocked.

'You have to be very careful here, not everything is as it seems to be,' said Clive, still smiling.

'Well how the hell are you supposed to know?' I asked.

'You'd soon find out if you put your hand up his skirt,' Clive replied.

'Oh good grief, that's it for me pal,' I said. 'Let's go back to The Landmark. I'll stick with the band!'

The next time I would encounter more of these 'Lady Men' would be a few days later on the island of Phuket.

Clive wanted to take Karla somewhere special and as she had never flown before, he chose Phuket.

Whisky had a few days off work at the same time, she also had never flown before, so I pulled out another credit card and off we went.

The flight was wonderful. It was everything a flight should be for someone who has never flown before. A famous 60's song lyric sprang to mind,

'I've looked at clouds from both sides now.'

The sky was a beautiful shade of blue with cotton wool clouds floating by, very gracefully, below us.

Whisky and Karla were elated by it all. They were behaving like a couple of kids let loose on a fairground ride. I enjoyed watching their reactions as through their eyes I looked at things in a fresh light. The plane circled low over the island of Phuket. The scene was magical. I had never seen such beauty. The colours of the forests and the translucence of the crashing seas made a myriad of hues. It invited the indulgences of pleasure. Whoops of delight accompanied our landing at the little airport. We clambered delightedly into a taxi.

It was quite a long journey, virtually the length of the island, but worth it when we finally saw our hotel. Set into the hillside, and surrounded by palm trees, it was fantasy land. For Whisky and myself the next three days would be like a honeymoon. I know we weren't married yet but what the hell, let's go for it!

Phuket is Thailand's fantasy southern island province in the Andaman Sea. Magnificent long white beaches with crystal blue sea water, luxuriant vegetation and breathtaking scenery in a calm tropical atmosphere made this an ideal place for us to unwind.

After the oppressive heat and pollution of Bangkok, Phuket was a joy with its balmy ocean breezes wafting through the coconut palms. It was a paradise where one felt only good things could happen. In the town there were massive open markets where exotic foods from Neptune's stores slithered and crawled in their freshness, where fruits looked larger and more succulent than I had ever seen.

I swam in the ocean between bouts of lying on the white sands with nothing more to think of than whether the coconut directly above my head would decide to fall at that moment or to choose another. From sand to sea I revelled in the wonder of it all. Whisky at one point ran into the sea towards me. She was fully clothed and she swam and splashed and giggled as we danced with bubbling joy in heaven. She had never been to the seaside before.

I had never felt so relaxed. I didn't want it to end. We talked to my children on the telephone and I pictured my house in England with grey skies overhead and the contrast was too much to countenance.

I was happy. We were happy. We were in the process of making memories. We were getting to know each other far away from the tensions of Bangkok.

Over the three days we were on Phuket I learned much more about Whisky, her family, her ex-husband and about her feelings toward me.

Her first husband was a shit! Sorry to be so direct, but any man that deserts a child he has fathered in my book is a shit. But this guy was a big shit! He not only deserted Whisky and her son, but took her to meet the girl he was deserting her for. This was done so that Whisky was able to see that the girl in question was, in his opinion, more beautiful than Whisky, and therefore justified his actions. Whisky's little boy was three months old.

On our second night in Phuket we decided to go to the theatre. If we had been in Blackpool it would probably have been 'Little and Large' but this was Thailand!

The Simon Cabaret is apparently world famous, or so Clive told me. Well I must have led a very sheltered life because I'd never heard of it. The theatre was wonderful, very modern and hi-tech. The show itself was not only well produced, well constructed and brilliantly performed, it was extremely disconcerting. We sat for two hours watching some of the most beautiful sexy women I had ever seen in my life, and they were all fellas. It must be something they put in the rice! How can men be that beautiful and feminine? Many of them had undergone operations to give them the required missing bits up top and this really upset Whisky.

'They are men Mike, and have bigger boob than me, life not fair.'

After the show we made our way outside amidst a throng

of people who seemed to share in the same sense of disbelief as we did. The land of the rising sun had arrived, with five cameras apiece. They stood in groups like miniature accordions and clicked away at the cabaret artists as they draped themselves in snappable poses while pretending this was not their purpose at all. A thousand eyes inverted them and camcorders whirred impertinently into every crevice of their forms. From beneath the borrowed eyes, fixed smiles, stamped out like happy face stickers chattered amazement at the feast of sights. Fan-like, the Cabaret programmes supported noses. Their paraphernalia dangled on straps like reins on forgotten children as they crammed into their rice bowl of sameness.

'Yukimasau, Michael-san. Exit stage left in a flurry,' thought Michael in an attempt to rediscover his karma.

On the way walking back to our hotel, Clive suddenly announced he wanted to go for a stroll on his own. The pressure of the situation he and Karla were in was really getting him down. The days were flying by and very soon he would be returning to England, alone again. Karla was very upset, she worshipped Clive. To Karla Clive was the legendary white knight on the white horse. Whisky sat with Karla on a bench overlooking the sea, trying to explain the pressure and frustration Clive was feeling. Of course Karla felt just as frustrated with the situation as Clive did. I don't know which was worse, having to sit around waiting for developments as Karla had to do, or to deal with all the paperwork and bureaucracy that was Clive's responsibility in England. It was hell for both of them. All Whisky and I could do was listen, sympathise and help where and when we could.

In a strange sort of way I was grateful to Clive and Karla for showing me what the future might have in store for me and Whisky. It certainly gave me incentive to research everything thoroughly in an effort to dispel any fears the British Embassy might have in regard to granting us a visa. Clive eventually returned having cleared his head, put his arm around Karla, apologised, and everything was all right again.

The next morning Whisky and I were to have a very serious chat about our own future. She agreed with me that it was
probably better to approach the Embassy engaged, not married.
I felt that if we were married we would be in some way demand-
ing a visa, however, if we were engaged we would be requesting
a visa. In my opinion all the Embassy wanted to see was an intelligent, unrushed, well thought out approach. In fact it was simple really, just stick to the truth. We knew we wanted to be together, however we weren't sure where we wanted to be together.
If Whisky was granted a visa to come to England, she might not
like it. I knew a little about Thailand but Whisky knew nothing
about England. So all we were asking the Embassy for was the
opportunity to find out where we wanted to live together. This
seemed sensible, and was in fact the case.

We also decided that we should wait a little longer before
we approached them, to give our relationship the added cred-
ibility of longevity.

'So how do we officially get engaged in Thailand?' I asked
Whisky, bearing in mind that she was Muslim, and I knew nothing about Muslims.

'We have party,' she replied.

'A party, what sort of party?' I responded.

'Just party for family and friends,' said Whisky. 'Make announcement we together. This make it official. It called 'married
at home' This what I do with ex-husband. Many do like this in
Thailand.'

'So you did not go through a civil ceremony with your ex-
husband?' I asked.

'No, just party. Many Thai couple do like this,' she repeated.

'So you were never officially married to him?' I asked to be
sure I was getting this right.

'No, just party,' she replied, a little impatiently.

'So you haven't got divorce papers, you can't have because
you were never legally married?' I was thinking out loud.

'No, just party,' she replied again slowly and with emphasis. She obviously thought I was being really slow to grasp this.

'Well that's good news. It's one piece of paper we won't
have to produce,' I said, rubbing my hands together.

'Where can we go to buy an engagement ring Whisky?' I asked.

'Buy engagement ring? Why? I don't need one,' she replied.

Don't you just love her? She still didn't need anything, but I was determined to put a ring on her finger, mainly to keep away the wolves at The Landmark. Eventually she agreed to let me buy her one but insisted that it did not need to be expensive. That's my girl!

Phuket was a dream but we had to wake up. The carefree fantasy island would have to fade. We faced the reality of our return to Bangkok.

The Thai jeweller we went to see was extremely kind and helpful. Whisky looked at many rings. She seemed really happy, and finally chose one.

'But it's black,' I said. She had chosen a simple gold ring with a black stone.

'Yes,' she said. 'Very beautiful.'

'But it's black,' I repeated with emphasis.

'I like black stone, very pretty,' she replied, holding her inverted hand up in the air.

'But you can't have a black engagement ring, it's supposed to be a diamond or a ruby, or a sapphire,' I informed her.

'Why? I like black stone,' she said with some determination.

The jeweller just looked on, nodding and smiling broadly with his hands clasped together. His eyes went to and fro, from Whisky to me and back again, as if he were watching a game of tennis.

'You said could choose what I wanted,' Whisky said.

'Well yes, but no one I know has ever chosen a black stone for an engagement ring,' I informed her.

'I be different from everyone then?' she asked.

'You certainly will,' I replied.

'I have black one then, I like be different,' she said with a sweet smile and definite finality in her voice.

So a black stone engagement ring it was to be.

Next we had to find a place to have the party and decide when it was to be. Whisky was now back at work on the night shift with no more days off before I returned to England. She therefore finished work at about two thirty in the morning.

'We have party after work on Friday,' she announced.

'At two thirty in the morning?' I asked in amazement. 'Who the hell is going to come to a party at two thirty in the morning? What about your mother and sisters?'

'Be all right, do not worry, this is Bangkok,' she replied reassuringly.

'Well where in Bangkok are you going to find a place to agree to house a party at two thirty in the morning?' I asked.

'Jim and Tor, Thai House, no problem,' she said smiling.

'Are you sure they will be willing to do this for us?' I asked.

'No, not sure,' she replied.

'Well we had better go and ask them,' I said, and so indeed we did.

I was about to find out that Jim Arthur, who I had met in The Huntsman, was a trooper.

'Bloody stupid time to have a party!' said Jim with some conviction.

'Anyway Tor and I usually go home on Friday's. Can't you have it another time?'

Jim and his Thai wife Tor lived at Thai House during the week but returned to their home, some way out of the city centre, at weekends.

I explained that Friday night was the only time we could do this as I was returning to England on the following Monday.

'But it's Thursday today, it doesn't give us much time to organise the food, and then there's the band. You'll need the band.'

He must have recognised the look on my face as desperate.

'Look,' he said, more encouragingly. 'Have a word with Tor about the sort of food you want, how many for and so on, and if we can do it we will.'

I could have kissed him. What a man! He didn't know me from Adam and he'd just agreed to put off going home for his weekend break so that we could have a piss up to announce our engagement.

Tor was realistic. She didn't ask us what we would like to eat at the party, she rather told us what she was able to do at such short notice. Personally I wasn't bothered, baked beans would have been fine. However Tor did a helluva lot better than baked beans. Thai House has an excellent reputation for traditional Thai food, which is very well deserved.

She was of course very impressed with me, Whisky's future husband. She said , 'Seems all right but talks too much.' A woman of discerning qualities to be sure.

While Whisky and Tor were finalising arrangements I talked to Jim. He gave me the benefit of his knowledge and wisdom of Thai ways and customs.

'You do realise what you are doing with this party thing, don't you Mike?'

'Getting engaged?' I offered as an answer and a question.

'Well not really Mike. You're basically getting married. You are standing in front of all her friends and family and making a statement that you and Whisky are an item, and I mean an item! Nothing legally binding of course, but nevertheless it will be accepted as a marriage between you.'

'Couldn't be happier then,' I replied with conviction.

'Well just so long as you know what you're doing,' Jim said seriously.

'Jim,' I said. 'I know little of Thai customs, and I feel that I've only just started to get to know Whisky. But I do know one thing for sure, I love her very much, and no matter what this country or the British Embassy throws up at me I will deal with it. I am not going to lose this lady for anything or anyone.'

Jim nodded and smiled, seemingly content with my outpourings of positive thinking.

'Should be a good night then,' he smiled knowingly. 'See you Friday.'

Now, as yet, I hadn't met Whisky's mother. We were supposed to meet her before we went to Phuket, but she didn't turn up. That inspired me with a lot of confidence I can tell you. Whisky said that she had probably forgotten. That inspired me with even less confidence. But I was assured that she would turn up for the party.

Whisky's two sisters, Janjira and Dongnapa, would not be able to be there. I can't remember why, but I'm sure there was a good reason. I hadn't at this stage been told much about these two sisters except that they were both younger than Whisky. Obviously Whisky's father wasn't going to be there as he still didn't know I existed. So the only member of the family that would be turning up would be my future mother- in -law and I would be meeting her for the first time. Oh boy!

Although things were proceeding according to plan there was still something nagging at me. We had worked our way through the doubts implanted by her friends, and I knew about the difficulty with her father being a strict Muslim, but there was still a piece of the jigsaw missing. The happy laid back girl I had first met was now more intense, more serious. She was often lost in her thoughts as if looking for answers to questions not fully formulated. I also began to wonder why I had not met more members of her family. I had so far only met her grandmother on my last trip. Clive had met all of Karla's family before his engagement. He had discussed the bridal price and made arrangements for the ceremony. I, on the other hand, had bought Whisky an inexpensive ring and a guitar. Whisky told me not to worry. She was Muslim. Things were different. I was not satisfied with this simple explanation.

So the night of the party arrived. The night that I thought I was getting engaged, the night that Thai culture thought I was getting married, the night that Whisky's father knew nothing about, and God knows what her mother thought we were doing.

Clive said not to worry about it because, if nothing else, it was a step in the right direction. Whisky was making a commitment, and in front of her mother and friends. Content with that belief, I relaxed a bit and started to look forward to the party.

Karla had been in bed all day with a very bad cold. She was, however, determined to be there for us and turned up with Clive at two o'clock sneezing violently. I had been at Thai House only a few minutes when they arrived. The food was all laid out on a large table in the centre of the restaurant. It looked wonderful, lots of different exotic dishes, none of which I recognised. We sat down with a drink each and waited.

At about two-forty-five people started to arrive, some of whom I recognised as Whisky's friends from The Huntsman. They told me Whisky was making herself look beautiful for me, and would be arriving very soon.

At three o'clock she appeared, looking really stunning in a long white evening dress. She really was the most beautiful girl I had ever seen, and I felt immensely proud of her.

'I thought you said you'd only got one dress,' I said, 'You look absolutely wonderful!'

She laughed and told me she'd been shopping with her mother that day. Right on cue her mother arrived in a taxi. Whisky introduced me and I said something along the lines of,

'Hi Mom, really good to meet you at last.'

An inspired opening statement I thought!

She gave me one of those looks perfected by mothers of girls and reserved for their boyfriends. I was suddenly feeling nervous again.

We all went into Thai House, the two piece band plus drum machine started to play, and the party got under way.

Everyone ate and drank for a while. I talked to Whisky's Mom for quite a long time, trying to convince her that I would make an excellent son-in-law! As her English was limited I wasn't at all sure that the message was getting across. I got the overall impression that she liked me, but it could have been indigestion. She looked quite a lot like Whisky having similar facial features, with the same lovely smile and gentle manner. I liked her very much.

Jim had very kindly given us a few bottles of champagne

as an engagement present. I told you he was a trooper, and everyone was given a glass for the toast.

But first the speeches, yes even in Thailand there had to be speeches.

Amando, the leader of the band from The Huntsman, wished us well on behalf of everyone present. I then had to respond.

Now it was not a bit of good getting deep and meaningful here with lots of big words to impress everyone how well educated I was, most of them only spoke a little English.

So I firstly thanked them all for coming, and asked Whisky to stand up. I showed them all the ring, I then put it on the appropriate finger, held her hand in the air and said, 'Together forever.' They all cheered, even her mother.

The party finally finished around seven o'clock in the morning after I had done some excellent impressions of Thai dancing, kick boxing, and elephants playing football. I blame the champagne and the fact that I was ecstatically happy.

We returned to our hotel after the last of the guests left Thai House. I managed to carry Whisky over the threshold to our room, goodness knows how as I was more than slightly inebriated. On this occasion it was Whisky's turn to put me to bed. All I can remember was giggling a lot as I had the hiccups.

Whisky and I were now officially engaged, or was it unofficially married. I still wasn't really sure. But we had made a commitment to each other, and were two very happy people.

14. Reviewing the Situation

Monday arrived far too quickly and it was time to head back to England again. Before we left for the airport we all met at The Huntsman for a farewell drink, Clive and Karla, Martin and Gow, myself and Whisky, who was of course working.

Martin had returned from northern Thailand where he had been to meet Gow's relations and to arrange their wedding. Wedding! That was quick! He doesn't hang about, our Martin! He was lucky in not having to approach the British Embassy for a visa. He had left England several months previously to live and work in Saudi Arabia. Martin had come to dislike England and maintained that he would never live there again. He had run his own small building company which had gone bankrupt during what he described as 'The Depressing Thatcher Years.' His view on Conservative Britain, whose policies he very firmly blamed for the collapse of his company, is not really publishable! He had once been married, but was now divorced and had no strong family ties to keep him in the UK. Vietnam was a country Martin thought he may well end up living and working in, but thought he would start off his new married life in Thailand.

Eventually we all said our goodbyes. Martin and Gow headed back to the hotel, Clive, Karla and I headed for the airport and Whisky stayed at The Huntsman to finish her shift.

At the airport Karla was in tears. Clive kept his composure in front of her until he was the other side of immigration control. He then sat down and quietly cried. He knew it would be a very long time before he was able to afford to return to Bangkok.

It was a sad scene. Although I could understand why the British Embassy had failed their application, I shared their grief, and I had to watch them suffer.

I knew that Whisky and I may have to go through the same anguish. It was not just the fact that they had to be apart, more the uncertainty of when, if ever, they would be allowed to be together. They really had fallen in love with each other over a very short period. The Embassy had judged this to be unsafe, and in most cases it probably would be. But in this case the Embassy had unfortunately got it wrong and it was very sad to watch the resulting distress that this decision had caused my friends.

It seemed a terribly long flight back to England this time. The fact that I wasn't able to sleep at all made it seem endless. When we did finally arrive at Manchester airport we took a taxi to Clive's home which took another hour. Then, after a quick cup of tea, I backed my car out of Clive's garage and headed for my home, a journey of over two hours. All in all I had been on the move for close on twenty four hours, and was understandably very tired.

Two days later trying to explain to Wilf that I was unofficially married was a hoot.

'Look Mick, you're either married or you ain't!' he said emphatically.

'It's not that simple Wilf, it's a cultural thing,' I said.

'Look Mick, if you split up does she get half yer house?'

'No Wilf,' I replied.

'Then you ain't married pal!' he said, more emphatically.

Wilf had very definite views on what he saw as the unfair legal aspects of marriage break ups.

He said to me once, while we were discussing the trauma a friend of ours was going through,

'They've gone over the top with this thing Mick. What men need to do now is go out and find a woman they utterly detest and buy her an house!'

To Wilf all things in life are either black or white. I would love one day to take him to Bangkok and just watch his reactions. It would be most entertaining, for the Thais as well as for me.

'So when are you going back to the land of the rising sun?' he asked.

'That's Japan Wilf,' I replied.

'Whatever Mick, whatever.'

'As soon as I can basically. Whisky is expecting me to go sometime in July.'

'What's Keith going to say about that? You're asking an awful lot of him you know. He's been working his short and curlies off while you've been in the land of the rising penis.'

'You're really basic at times Wilf,' I replied.

'I don't care Mick. It's got to be addressed. You don't want to lose all your friends, do you?'

He was absolutely right of course, I had pushed my friendship with Keith to the limit. Something would have to be arranged, or I would not only lose a friend but an excellent business partner to boot.

The solution was presented to me a few days later when I was explaining my dilemma to another friend of mine called Phil.

'It's simple Mike,' he said. 'Why use one friend when you can use two, I'll help Keith to run the company when you go back to Bangkok.'

At this time Phil wasn't working. He had gone through a very difficult period following redundancy. It was an ideal solution, he could earn a bit of money and I would be able to return to Thailand content in the knowledge that the company was in good hands.

Phil had, right from the start, been utterly supportive of my trips to Thailand. We are very similar in character, and he always understood what I was doing, and why I was doing it.

My children were still a tower of strength to me and utterly supportive. They spoke several times to Whisky on the telephone and couldn't wait to meet her.

My ex-wife however was not so understanding. Three trips to Thailand, three times she had to look after the children. In her opinion I was messing them about, which she felt was not good for them. The children didn't see it this way, but to be fair she did have a point. The situation could not go on for ever, it was disrupting people's lives, both family and friends, every time I went to Thailand.

I made my ex-wife a promise in that when I returned from the next trip I would very definitely be able to inform her what my future had in store.

At the time this was a very rash promise. I had no idea what my life was going to do, it all depended on the British Embassy in Bangkok.

I sat down and reflected on where I had been, where I was now, and where I was going. I even wrote things down to help me assess the situation I was in, something I very rarely do. There were just so many unanswered questions floating about at the front of my mind.

What if the Embassy didn't grant us a visa?

There was no way I could keep travelling backwards and forwards to Thailand, I just couldn't afford it.

Was our relationship strong enough to undergo long separations?

I certainly hoped so, but by no means was I one hundred percent sure.

Would I contemplate going to live in Thailand if the worst came to the worst?

This would be a direct choice between Whisky and my children and to be honest I couldn't at this time come up with an answer. Clive was certainly contemplating it as a solution to his forced separation from Karla.

I weighed up the plusses and minuses. Certainly, I had found the lady I wanted to marry and to spend my life with. Was I going to be able to? The clouds of the British Embassy loomed grey over our happiness. I had doubts which ate away at me; doubts which would not go away. They festered and grew.

15. Up is Down and Down is Up

I had planned to return to Bangkok in July and had made an appointment at the British Embassy for us to be interviewed. I had sent all the documents that the Embassy required prior to the interview but knew that there were other documents that would have to be produced at the interview itself. Some of these documents were in Thai, Whisky's birth certificate for instance, and would need to have an English translation attached to them. Whisky would also have to get herself a passport and we would need to produce letters written to each other during our relationship, with proof of posting dates. The pile of my letters to Whisky would be large compared to the three letters I had received from her. I hoped this would not be seen by the Embassy as unbalanced. I even looked out all my telephone bills to prove that we had spoken many times on the telephone, as compensation for the lack of correspondence from Whisky.

From talking to the Thai Embassy in London, and immigration departments in Birmingham and London, it became clear that we would also need documents relating to Keyowan's situation.

The overall plan agreed with Whisky before I left Bangkok was to approach the British Embassy for a fiancee visa to allow her to visit England to see whether she wished to live here permanently. If it transpired that she did, we would then marry in England and return to Bangkok to request a visa for her son to join us.

There was no way that the Embassy were going to grant us a visa for Whisky unless we could prove that she had sole custody of her son, and that he would be well looked after until we returned to get him. None of this could be done in England. It had to be done in Bangkok. It became apparent that I was going to have to return to Thailand sooner than originally planned. Jim had told me how long this type of thing could take, Thai bureaucracy being well known for its lack of urgency. He had even suggested that a few back-handers may be necessary to quicken the production of the documents we needed. Nothing illegal, just oiling the works.

There was only one solution to all this. I would have to go back earlier to allow time for all this documentation to be done. There was no way that Whiskey could do it on her own. She worked long hours and would not have the time.

Suddenly, I had a thought. I would go back to bangkok earlier than expected, but not tell whiskey. I would surprise her.

Jim had suggested I stay at Thai house on my return, and had promised to do me a good deal on accomodation charges.

I telephoned to tell Jim the date I would be arriving and asked him to tell Whiskey that it was vital she be at Thai House at twelve noon on that day to receive a call from me in England, as I had important information to tell her. The plan was that I would actually be telephoning from my room in Thai House. Whiskey would think that she was speaking to me in England. I would then ask her to hold on while I let the dog out or something, then I would go down to reception, creep up behind her, and surprise her.

It all went according to plan. I arrived at Thai House at nine o'clock in the morning and went for a sleep in my room. Jim telephoned me at five to twelve to tell me that Whisky had arrived. I telephoned reception and Jim handed the telephone to Whisky. I asked her to hang on, rushed down to reception, crept up behind her and said,
'Hello darling.'
She dropped the phone, went very pale, looked at Jim who was laughing, looked back at me, and laughed.
'Mike, you are devil,' she said.
'I know,' I replied. 'Good isn't it?'

Jim got us both a drink and we sat chatting until Whisky had to go to work at five o'clock that afternoon. She was still on the night shift. I had brought my small computer with me so that I could, at least, do some work for my company during my absence. I would now be in Bangkok for five weeks, during which my status would change. Slowly I would cease to feel like a tourist and start to look on this enigmatic city as a second home.

Whisky and I lived together in my room at Thai House for this entire period. She told her father that she was staying with her mother.

The whole situation with regard to her father not knowing anything about our relationship, really bothered me. I did not like the fact that Whisky, and the rest of her family for that matter, were having to lie to him.

Jim took me under his wing. He recognised that I was genuine in my feelings for Whisky but knew nothing of Thai ways. He also recognised the fact that I wanted to learn and very much wanted to understand. I have never been one to believe that British ways are necessarily best just because I happen to be British.

Jim's opinion on the situation with regard to Whisky's father was that it was best left to the women of the family. He believed that I had nothing to fear as they would protect me at all costs. In his opinion the missing jigsaw piece was all to do with the father and the Muslim faith.

'You have been accepted by Whisky's mother who recognises your genuine feelings for her daughter, so leave it alone. They will deal with it in their own way. There are things you can do in Bangkok and things that you can't. This is one to leave well alone,' Jim said with a fair degree of conviction. I took his advice.

Jim would have many talks with this ignorant Englishman over the next few weeks. His advice was invaluable and given freely as a friend.

'Be careful here Mike,' Jim continued. 'Bangkok has a habit of lulling you into a sense of false security and then biting you in the bum when you least expect it. Never let anger be your first emotion. Stand back, go into lateral thinking mode, assess each situation carefully. The Thais have been doing things in their own special way for over two thousand years and they're not about to change it for anyone, including you. Often you won't understand them, or how they do things, and often you will feel very frustrated. However it works, God knows why, but it does work for them.'

'You really know this place and the people well Jim,' I offered as a compliment.

'Mike,' he said with an air of frustration. 'I have lived in this country for ten years and I'm still only scratching the surface of trying to understand them. In your room you have a light switch, haven't you?'

'Yes Jim,' I replied, wondering what the hell that had to do with anything.

'Have you noticed anything different about it compared to the west?' he asked.

'You mean it's backwards,' I answered. 'On is off, and off is on?'

'Exactly!' he replied, smiling broadly. 'That's your starting point in understanding Thais.'

Deep, I thought, very deep.

'Don't ever expect a Thai to turn up on time. It rarely happens. They'll blame the traffic, the weather, or anything that comes to mind. I'm in business here. Thais that I deal with have had to accept that there are two sorts of time, Bangkok time and Jim's time. It has taken a long while to get that across to them but now it seems to be working better.'

This man was going to be so useful to me. I bought him a beer.

Thai House had a unique quality about it, one always felt utterly at home there. From the outside it looks a little bit like a Swiss chalet. Inside, the large open plan ground floor area, includes a restaurant with a bar and a small stage area for the two-piece band plus drum machine. At the far end there is the reception area where one checks in.

The receptionist was a Thai man called Mr. Ort who was always very helpful and seemed to work there twenty four hours a day. He slept when he could in a little office behind the reception desk. Often when Whisky and I returned in the early hours of the morning we could hear Mr. Ort snoring and see his legs sticking out of the open office door.

Thai House was an eastern copy of Fawlty Towers. Jim even looked like John Cleese and he dealt with his staff in the same manner. There was even an equivalent Manuel, a young Thai boy who always got things wrong. When I asked him for a cup of tea, he looked at me in the same vacant manner until I used the Thai word 'chalon' and then he would leap into action but forget to bring any sugar and milk. A cup with a floating tea bag would arrive. Jim would take him behind the bar, cuff him around the ears, put a sugar bowl and milk jug into his hands and kick him up the bum for good measure. It was a bit of playacting put on by Jim for entertainment.

Jim's wife Tor was much more serious as she went about her work. She ran the place basically and did it very well. Most of the staff were related in some way. Her mother did most of the shopping and her father was the chef. Away from work Tor would let her hair down and enjoy herself. She was a lovely lady and so attractive. I had found the best place to stay in Bangkok. I could not have wished for better.

16. The Phantom Bangkok Bum Biter

When Keith, Phil and I put on musicals with our youth theatre group in our home town we used to have them videoed. The delightful man who used to do this for us was called Eric. He was retired, had heart problems, but also had more energy than someone half his age. He was always there when you needed him, always did a great job, and never charged us very much for doing it. I had kept Eric up to date along the way with regard to my adventures in Bangkok, and he was always supportive and interested. One day he telephoned me and asked me to provide him with photos, in date order, with comments on the back, of my travels. He said he had just got himself some new computer software and wanted to test it out. Within a few days he returned all the pictures plus a video. All my photographs were now on the video, in date order, with all the comments I had added, plus music I had written as background. It was mine and Whisky's story, a video record of our relationship. What a great surprise this was, and I knew Whisky would be very touched by it.

I chose one evening, after we had been out for an Indian meal, to take Whisky to the first hotel I had stayed in where I knew they had a video player in reception. I was fairly sure that my little friend Jym, the receptionist, would let us use it so that Whisky could watch Eric's epic.

We arrived at the hotel about midnight. Jym was very pleased to see us both, and was kind enough to let us use the video player as there was no one in reception at that late hour.

Whisky watched the video all the way through. She was obviously touched by it as the tears welled up. From the photo Whisky had first sent me to our trip to Siam Park, our hotel, Phuket and our engagement party at Thai House, it was all on the video.

Eric had also cleverly superimposed both our faces appropriately in whisky glasses and the whole presentation was accompanied by my music in the background. Whisky loved it and her gratitude showed in her glowing face. I was so grateful to Eric. He had helped me to show Whisky how much importance I attached to all that we had done together. It helped to cement our relationship.

Life very quickly fell into a sort of routine. When Whisky was at work, I worked on my computer. When she wasn't we were shooting around Bangkok sorting out all the documents that we needed for The Embassy.

As we were waiting at one of the offices for a translation to be done Whisky said that her stomach hurt and she thought it was probably the ghost.

'You think it's what?' I asked, to make sure I'd heard her correctly.

'Ghost in my stomach,' she repeated.

We had spoken many times of spirits, things that go bump in the night, and inexplicable happenings. Thailand is over ninety percent Buddhist and spirits are a central part of this religion. Outside every dwelling and business you will see a little model house stuck on top of a pole. This is so that the spirits have somewhere to live. Every day flowers, food and drink are placed in these little houses to keep the spirits happy. Jim Arthur had told me many stories of the magical and mysterious east. Even so I couldn't believe that Whisky really thought she had spirits in her stomach causing her distress.

'Where has this ghost come from?' I asked her, trying not to sound disbelieving.

'Last night, I think I eat too much ghost,' she replied.

'Whisky, you can't eat ghosts, don't be silly,' I said.

'We did Mike, you too, we eat chicken, beef and ghost, but ghost no good.'

It then dawned on me what this was all about. She called lamb, goat, and with her pronunciation it sounded like ghost.

I also spent a lot of time in The Huntsman Pub reading books and listening to the band. I was a happy man, everything was progressing smoothly, and I was content in my false sense of security. Then suddenly the Phantom Bangkok Bum Biter, the one that Jim had warned me about, grabbed my arse!

I had arrived at The Huntsman Pub on this particular evening, sat at my usual table, and ordered a beer. As Whisky brought it across to me I could see from the expression on her face that something was wrong.

'Mike, if I go to England can I get job?' she asked.

'Yes if you want to,' I replied. 'What sort of job, waitressing?'

'It doesn't matter. How much I earn?'

'What's this all about Whisky? You look really worried.'

'Dad must move from house, can't look after my son any more. Ma will look after but will need help, only earn little money. How much they pay in England?'

She then had to attend to another customer.

'We'll talk later,' I said. 'Don't worry.'

I waited till Whisky finished work and walked with her back to Thai House. We sat on the bed and she told me the extent of the problem.

Where she lived with her father was rented and the landlord had an offer to sell the property for redevelopment. There was no way that Whisky or her father could buy a house, he didn't work and Whisky had no money. The only solution seemed to be that Whisky's mother should look after the little boy until he could come to England. But no one knew for sure that Whisky would be going to England, let alone her little boy. It was all a bit of a mess.

What made it even more difficult was the fact that Whisky's mother lived in a one room apartment with not enough space to swing the proverbial cat.

She would have to find somewhere else to live.

If this had been England I would have had no problem sorting all this out, but this was Bangkok and I had no idea where to start.

The next day Whisky shot off to talk to her mother. I went downstairs to talk to Jim. I desperately needed some advice.

'Fancy a beer Jim?' I asked.

'Problem already?' he replied knowingly.

I told him the situation we found ourselves in. He listened, nodding occasionally.

'It's very simple really Mike. You've got to buy a house.' He could see my shock, horror, disbelief.

'You'd better have another beer.' He called the waiter over.

'You see Mike, Whisky is the oldest child of the family, she's responsible for her parents. There's no pension plans or social security here, all Thai children are brought up with the understanding that they will have to look after their parents in old age.'

'But neither of her parents are old Jim,' I stated.

'It doesn't matter in this case because the situation amounts to the same thing. Her father cannot work because of a back injury and her mother has a very low paid job. There is no way that Whisky will leave her family in this situation. It has to be sorted out, and the only person who can sort it out is you. If Whisky was staying in Thailand her job at The Landmark would solve the problem, it's not a badly paid number. But who is going to keep the family if Whisky leaves the country? She is the oldest child. In Thailand that makes it her responsibility. As I said the only solution here is that you buy a house.'

'Oh well put like that Jim it is simple, as you say, all I've got to do is buy a house. But with what Jim, I've not got that sort of money.'

'You're thinking as a westerner again Mike. This is Thailand. It's not as bad as you think,' Jim said, with that all knowing smile again.

'So spell it out for me my friend because at the moment it certainly feels as bad as I think it is,' I replied, trying to hold on to a little bit of dignity.

'Houses here are not as expensive as you might think. You can buy a small house, or apartment for as little as ten thousand pounds. It all depends of course where they wish to live. If you can raise the deposit, say around one thousand, you can have a mortgage for the balance. Interest rates in Thailand are lower than in England.'

This was sounding better. Thirty minutes ago I had a ton weight pressing on my head, now I only had two bags of cement.

'I know Whisky quite well Mike. She won't ask you to do this. She hasn't ever asked you for anything, has she? Not like a lot of girls I know of in this city. It is up to you whether you offer help or not. But if you don't I can't see her leaving Bangkok.'

'I understand what you're saying Jim, and I agree that it's down to me to give this help. The problem is one thousand pounds is a lot of money when you haven't got it.'

'When you marry a Thai, Mike, you marry her family, they're one and the same thing. Look at it this way. Whisky is giving up a hell of a lot more than you are. She is willing to leave her family, friends, job and her little boy, to go to a country she doesn't know, a culture she won't understand, and all on the strength of you telling her it will be 'all right on the night' Don't you think that's a lot to give, because it's everything she has. And into the bargain she'll probably freeze to death in the British winter. All you've got to give is one thousand pounds. I think you've got the better end of the deal personally.'

He was absolutely right of course. I knew the responsibility I was taking on with regard to Whisky's family some time ago. I had talked a lot to Clive about this aspect of marrying a Thai. (Remember the Bell for the Temple?) I was giving up nothing compared to Whisky. I would be in my own country surrounded by my own family. It was just the financial side of the equation that needed sorting out. I couldn't go into more debt, I was way over my limit as it was. Credit cards are easy to get, and even easier to use, but the piper has to be paid.

I went back to my room to think. Who could I ask to lend me a grand. Wilf couldn't, he was always broke, it was a way of life for him. Phil couldn't, he was on the dole. Keith might be a possibility, I rang him.

'You know the time to go away, don't you?' said Keith on the other end of the line.

'Have you got some problems then?' I asked with obvious concern.

'Yes,' said Keith. 'Keeping up with all the bloody orders. It's gone crazy since you left for Bangkok. Business has more than doubled on last year.'

I must have a guardian angel I thought to myself. I need money, and suddenly I've got money. Thank you, thank you, thank you.

I explained to Keith the situation I was in and he, supportive as ever, agreed to let the company fund the problem, as long as I bought him a bottle of his favourite Malt on my way back to England. Good deal, good friend.

I went back downstairs to tell Jim the good news.

'Where there's a will there's a way, even in Bangkok,' he said. 'You look as though you could do with a night on the town. How do you fancy going to see a few bands around the hotels?'

As Whisky wasn't returning until the following day it seemed like a great idea to me. Jim was right, I certainly felt the need to unwind.

17. The 'Dead Men Band' and Beyond

'First we'll go to The Ambassador,' said Jim. 'They've got a couple of good Filipino bands there. Then to a bar I know where the music is very loud. Finally we'll go to a night club and I'll show you the Dead Men Band.'

'The what?' I asked intrigued.

'You'll see,' he replied mysteriously.

Night time in Bangkok just happens. There's no warning and no gradual fading of the daytime light as in the west. At about six o'clock, every evening, someone draws the curtains on the day and suddenly you realise it's dark. Bangkok starts to change it's character with this loss of daytime light. As the sun disappears it is replaced by millions of twinkling and flashing neon lights enchanting and enticing you to sample what's on offer. Bangkok, the religious city with Sodom and Gomorrah within easy walking distance of any temple. At night the city of work and temples becomes the city of fun and frolic.

However the loss of the visible sun unfortunately doesn't mean much loss of heat. For people like myself, unused to this constant feeling of living in a greenhouse, it can be very oppressive. Thai people move very slowly in comparison to their western counterparts, which isn't at all surprising. Bangkok is a twenty four hour city and twelve hour work shifts are the norm for most people. Very few places close and so you can buy virtually anything you wish at any time. One is constantly bombarded with offers of services or goods, day and night, as one walks through the city. Apparently there isn't a Thai word for no, but a shake of the head seems widely understood and usually accepted.

We had a great night. Jim was well known in that area of Bangkok and we were treated with great respect everywhere we went. I felt special, I wasn't treated as a tourist, I was the friend of Mr. Jim and therefore accepted without question.

The Ambassador Hotel was as large, if not larger, than The Landmark Hotel where Whisky worked. As we entered the bar the band were setting up. We were shown to a table, sat down, and ordered some beer.

Eventually the band started to play. They were really amazing. I had now seen two bands in Bangkok, one at The Huntsman Pub and this one here. Both were Filipino, and both were excellent. The standard of musicianship was very high. If you closed your eyes you could see the original band whose song they were covering. I had experienced this in Japan a few years earlier. Eastern musicians copied western pop music so accurately that you couldn't spot the difference. I would have liked to hear some original material to assess their full potential, but that was not what they were paid to produce. I know musicians, and I know they must have been frustrated doing cover versions, but to look at them perform you would not know it. They were so very professional.

The second band we saw, who took over from the first, were Thai. They were different to the Filipino's, a different style of music heavily influenced by Thai folk traditions, but just as good. I was impressed. I had not expected the bands in Bangkok to be as good as in England, but in fact they were in many ways better than most I had seen.

We didn't stay long at the next place Jim took me to. The band there were good, but far too loud. I must be getting old. So on to the night club to see the Dead Men Band. It was only a small club, but cosy. The stage was empty as we sat down at one of the tables, the band were on their break. When they eventually walked on to the stage I understood completely why Jim called them The Dead Men Band. They looked dead. There were three of them, all fairly old, all very thin featured, and all looked skeleton like. This impression was accentuated when they started to play. They all looked as if they were about to fall over. You could just about see their fingers move over their instruments, but you had to concentrate really hard. It was weird, bodily they hardly moved a muscle. Rigor Mortis had obviously set in years before and they were doing their best to cope with it. However the sound they produced, playing old standards, was not at all bad.

We finished the night off at The Huntsman Pub. Whisky wasn't there of course. She was still with her mother. By the time we arrived the band had finished for the night and were sitting at a table having a well deserved drink. Jim and I joined them. They were lovely people. I had spoken to them all, but only briefly. They had all attended our engagement party where Amando, the groups leader, had toasted us. Amando was married to Sheila, the older of the two girl singers. I had a lot to thank Sheila for because at the time when most of Whisky's friends at The Huntsman were causing her grief about me, Sheila was telling Whisky not to take any notice of them as, in her opinion, I seemed to be a really nice and genuine guy.

Dante was the drummer and his sister, Rubette, was the younger girl vocalist. Dante's girlfriend Jubjang was one of Whisky's friends at the Huntsman Pub. Finally there was Frank. Dear old Frank. He didn't say a lot, usually seen accompanied by a beer glass when he wasn't playing keyboards. Together they were know as 'Mixed Beat'.

They told me that their contract with The Landmark would finish fairly soon and so they were looking for another place to play. They all had families back in the Philippines to support and so finding a new job was foremost on their minds. As they were an excellent band I was sure they would find work very soon.

We had a lot in common. We were all musicians and all foreigners in Thailand. Dante was also constantly being bitten by the Phantom Bangkok Bum Biter, so we used to swap horror stories.

Good friends, good music, good food. What more could a man ask for? I was, for the first time in Bangkok, feeling relaxed.

18. Unto Me a Son is Given

Whisky turned up the following day with her son who, I was informed, would be staying with us for a few days. Now there is a lot of difference between putting on a cabaret act for a day at Siam park and baby-sitting a three year old for hours who doesn't speak the same language. More of that in a minute.

I told Whisky of my solution to her family problems.

'No way Mike, forget it,' she said very firmly.

'But it's the only way you will be content to leave Bangkok,' I suggested.

'Are you rich man, money no problem?' she said quite angrily.

'Well no, I'm not rich, but I am able to do this,' I assured her.

'No way Mike, not fair, not your problem,' she repeated.

I tried again.

'In England Whisky when two people are married everything they have is shared. In the marriage service it says 'What's mine is yours, and what's yours is mine, very simple really.'

'But I haven't got anything Mike, so not fair. This my problem.'

Firmness needed I thought.

'No it's not just your problem. We are going to be married. That means sharing in everything both good and bad. I need to talk to your mother about this. When can I see her?' I was not taking no for an answer.

Whisky finally agreed to a meeting with her mother. It took a lot longer than the account above to convince her that it was the right thing to do. It also took just as long to convince her mother, but in the end it was decided that as a family we would buy a house. I would do my part, and they would do theirs. A solution was needed and a solution was found, that both cultures could live with.

I knew from the moment I saw Whisky's son that to marry her would be a package deal, so to speak. Love me, love my son. No other way really.

Whisky knew that I needed to get to know him better and so one night dropped me right in the deep end without any water wings.

She was getting ready to go to work. Kevin, as we now called him, was playing with some little toy cars I had bought for him.

'Is your Mom coming round for Kevin then?' I asked hopefully.

'No, you look after,' she replied, and carried on drying her hair.

'But he won't understand anything I say to him Whisky,' I said in desperation.

'You will manage,' she said smiling sweetly, put her things into her bag, kissed me, kissed Kevin and was gone.

Oh good grief! I didn't even know how to ask him if he wanted the toilet!

Also the little boy I had met at Siam Park was very well behaved. The one sitting on the floor in front of me was extremely naughty. He must, like me, have been on his best behaviour at the park, which he certainly wasn't now.

I tried to play with him, but he just kept throwing his toy cars at my head. I tried giving him some crisps, which he emptied on to the floor. I tried to take him to the toilet, and he piddled all over my trousers. I very quickly got the impression that this kid was testing me. It was all in his eyes, he knew exactly what he was doing.

I finally lost my patience, picked him up with my hands under his armpits, looked him straight in the eyes and said something very sternly along the lines of,

'Look Kevin, you've got two choices. You either be a good boy for Mike, or die!'

He didn't understand a word. He just put his thumb in his mouth, sucked it, and looked at me silently for ages. He was weighing me up.

It must have been something in the tone of my voice that

it, but that kid didn't put a foot wrong for the rest of the evening until he fell asleep. We played together, had a water fight in the bathroom, and then went downstairs for something to eat. He was as good as gold. On returning to the room I got him ready for bed, told him a story that he didn't understand, during which he fell to sleep.

I had learned something about this little Thai boy. He was a very bright child, and when he was good he was good, and when he was bad he was awful. So Kevin was a normal kid, thank goodness for that!

Whisky returned later from work.

'Has Kevin been a good boy?' she asked. 'Did you have any problem?'

'No problems at all,' I lied. 'We understand each other very well.'

Whisky laughed knowingly, and we all slept in the big double bed.

I had a new son.

19. The Beast That Had to Be Slain

Something was niggling at my insides. My willing acceptance of the fact that Whisky had presented me with a ready-made Kevin had been resolved and was obviously a major hurdle in her mind. There was something else. Back in England two months ago, just before my trip with Clive, I had sensed a change of attitude when Whisky and I had spoken on the phone. During that stay in Bangkok and then Phuket she had somewhat convinced me that what was worrying her was the pressure from her friends and her family problems. I still felt this was not the whole story.

I found it impossible to sleep in the heat. It seemed worse at night and too many thoughts occupied my head, especially the forthcoming interview at the Embassy. After watching the family of cats, in the alley below our room, try to negotiate their evening meal with the local rodent population, I sat on the floor amidst all the paperwork and the letters that Whisky and I had exchanged. She slept peacefully - angelic.

I carefully arranged the letters into an orderly paper rug. One caught my eye because, like a piece of a jigsaw, it didn't fit. One glance told me it was a love letter - but not from me.

It was from a guy in Hong Kong called Randy. The date on the letter meant that Whisky had received it about the time I started to notice a change in her manner on the telephone. It pronounced undying love and promises to return to see her again.

It hit me like a ton of proverbial house bricks. My heart started to pound, and I felt sick. This was the beast. I had found the rival I had always feared may exist. Clive and I had spoken many times about what had caused the change in Whisky's manner, and one of the reasons we came up with was exactly this, another man.

My ability to find humour in most things I have encountered in life just didn't work for me here. This wasn't funny, this meant at best I had been lied to. I paced the room for a while thinking what to do. I thought of Jim's advice, 'Never let anger be your first emotion.' But I was angry! All the journeys I had made to Bangkok, for what! I had got engaged to a girl I loved more than anyone I had ever known, but now to be confronted with this, another man in her life. Devastating!

'I hope to God nothing goes wrong because you'll never get over it, never,' Wilf's now prophetic words rang loudly in my ears.

So no humour to be found here I'm afraid, just a sad, angry and dejected man!

I gently shook Whisky's shoulder. She turned over, but did not wake. I then shook her more forcibly! She stirred,

'What on earth the matter Mike?' she asked, still not fully awake.

'What's this?' I asked, waving the letter in front of her face.

'What's what, darling?' she replied trying hard to focus on the waving piece of paper.

'Don't you darling me,' I said. 'Who the hell is Randy, when he's at home?'

'When he's where dear?' she replied, rubbing her eyes.

'Come on Whisky, wake up. Who is Randy, I insist you tell me what's being going on!'

'You're shaking again Mike,' she said as she took hold of the letter. She looked at it for a few moments, laughed and said,

'I'm sorry Mike you were not to see this. I have many letter from western man like this. He old. Many write letter to me at Huntsman. I throw them away.'

'Well you didn't throw this one away, did you! Why keep it Whisky? Have you any idea what reading it did to me?

It could, I supposed, be as she said. There were bound to be other admirers. She probably did have offers. She did work in a hotel. As if reading my mind she said, 'All girls at Huntsman get letter. They mean nothing.'

So why keep it for goodness sake?' I heard myself repeating.

'Do not know I had. Don't worry, it not important now. We

engaged, so why you worry?'

I was mollified to some degree. The flames that raged assuaged but a glow of doubt remained in the embers. No more was said. There was now a discernible tension between us. Whisky turned over and went back to sleep. I returned to the window and watched again the alley cats.

The flame still flickered. It was no good pretending. There was still a question mark wedged between our lips as we kissed when Whisky left for work.

I had to know. There had been a look on Whisky's face, when she first took hold of the letter, that I recognised. It was fear, the fear of discovery. I looked at the Hong Kong telephone number at the top of the letter for ages. I picked up the phone three times only to replace it again. I wanted to know but was frightened of knowing. I knew that if I did nothing it would just eat away at me. I picked up the receiver for a fourth time and dialled the number.

A woman answered and I asked who I was speaking to. She gave me her name and I asked to speak to her husband. The voice that answered did not sound like an old man. The flames licked under my tongue. My mouth felt dry. My hand shook.

'Am I speaking to Randy?'

He confirmed he was Randy.

'I'm sorry for bothering you so early in the morning, but do you know a girl in Bangkok called Whisky?'

There was a silence. He then confirmed that he did.

'Well I am engaged to Whisky. I have read your letter and am somewhat concerned as to the relationship you had, or perhaps still have, with my fiancee. I wonder if you would care to comment on this?'

His reply was tiptoed softly. It was obvious his wife hovered nearby. He told me he had taken Whisky out to a Disco when he was last in Bangkok and confirmed that he had written her the letter.

'And that is all that happened?' I asked.

'Yes I assure you. Look I am returning to Bangkok in a few days. Perhaps we could meet.'

'I can see no reason for us to meet,' I said somewhat taken aback. 'Did Whisky know that you were married Randy?'

'I have to go now,' came the hurried response, and the phone went dead.

So now I knew. It was not really earth shattering. Just a little shit let loose in Bangkok well away from the reach of his wife. But I was still concerned to know why Whisky had lied to me. Was it just a Disco, or was there more. It's like a disease isn't it, doubt.

That evening I told Whisky about my conversation with Randy, especially the bit about his wife.

Whisky's face screwed up in distress and she began to weep uncontrollably. She took from her finger the engagement ring and quiveringly handed it to me.

'I so sorry Mike, I lie to you, I so sorry.'

'You didn't know he was married did you Whisky?'

'No he tell me he single and he say he very much in love with me.'

The sound of a cars horn in the distance accentuated my pain and like a hurt animal I lashed out.

'So what I'm being asked to believe here is a guy pops into the Huntsman, swears undying love for you over a Singha beer, and whisks you off to a Disco to celebrate. Come on Whisky, don't insult my intelligence. How long was this little romance going on for while I was pining away on my own in England.'

'OK Mike. I tell you whole truth. You sure you want to know? You will only get upset.' She had stopped crying now and sounded annoyed.

'He come in Huntsman every night for two week. He send me many flower. He tell me he love me. He tell me he single. He no look at anyone but me.'

'He doesn't know Martin does he?' I asked, remembering the advice given to me on my first visit to the Huntsman.

'Pardon?' she replied.

'Oh, never mind, go on,' I said.

'I say I no go out with him and he get very drunk.'

'Ah, he definitely doesn't know Martin then,' I replied.

'Mike, why you keep talk about Martin?' she asked.

'Doesn't matter,' I said. I'll tell you later.'

'My friends at Huntsman tell me he good guy, no marry like you, no chance me be second wife. One night all of waitress go to disco and ask him to go with me. So I go with him. I very confused. But we have nice time, and he very nice to me. I feel so stupid girl now. He really nasty man. He lie to me about wife,' she started to cry again.

'Did you really like him then?' I asked.

'Yes, he all right, but I get very confused. I feel very lonely. I not sure you come back. Friends say you no come back again. Now I think I very foolish girl.'

I put my arm around her.

'I ruin everything,' she said, still sobbing.

'Not necessarily Whisky. But do I now know the whole truth? Are there any beasts left to slay? Are there any more skeletons to emerge from Thai cupboards?' I asked.

'No more Mike, but now too late, I ruin everything.'

'You haven't ruined anything you silly girl, I only wanted to know the truth. I love you too much to loose you now, especially over some little shit from Hong Kong. And I really dislike some of your so called friends. They haven't exactly given you good advice have they! But it's all over now, and we can get on with our life, hopefully with no more problems.'

So come on Whisky, stop crying, dry your eyes, and let me put the ring back on your finger.'

Her face showed utter disbelief.

'You still want me? I lie to you. Why you still want me? Thai man would not want me if I lie to him.'

'I am not a Thai man! I love you and I always will love you. Let's just stick to the truth from now on. Okay?'

Whisky stopped crying, nodded her head, and let me put the ring back on her finger.

She gave me a big kiss, told me she loved me, and I felt very relieved that the beast was now well and truly dead.

'Oh is he!' chortled the Phantom Bangkok Bum Biter.

Two nights later I was sitting in the Huntsman reading yet another book and truth to say protecting my interest when Whisky flew past me in a great hurry and out into the arcade. I couldn't see where she had gone. Then one of the waitresses, Jubjang, came over and said, 'Mike, Randy is outside.'

I got up quickly and went out into the arcade. I could see Whisky now talking to a man. She looked seriously angry. My attention was on the man, Randy.

I felt a sense of relief. He looked like a male version of the Russian women's lib activist I had met back in England. As a rival he was very disappointing. I had him pictured differently - tall, dark and handsome. Funny how the jealous mind can play tricks. He was in fact smaller than me with mousy coloured hair, and wore a tee shirt that closely resembled a green anorak favoured by such liberals. I walked straight over to where they were talking.

'You're Mike,' he said. The Aussie accent was unmistakable. Another goddam sheep-shearer I thought.

'I thought you would be here,' he began. 'I have come to apologise. I feel very embarrassed about all this.'

'Bollocks!' I thought, you've come to make sure we ain't going to tell your wife what you get up to in Bangkok.

'As I told you on the phone, there isn't a problem. I was not engaged to Whisky when you took her out. I only contacted you to establish that your association with Whisky was over. There are no hard feelings, I can assure you,' I said while wishing to choke him to death on the spot.

I offered instead to shake his hand in civilised fashion but he refused saying that he was too embarrassed. He said goodbye, wished us well, and made a hasty exit.

Whisky was fuming.

'He really nasty person,' she said. 'Why he no shake your hand? You offer him your hand. Why he no shake. Him nasty!'

'Obviously not British my dear. No style!' I joked with Whisky in my best Oxford accent, and we went back into the pub laughing.

Funny isn't it? What could have been a disaster ended up

drawing us closer together.

Jim's words of advice came to mind again.

'Never let anger be your first emotion.'

Sorry uncle Jim, but I'm only human.

Somewhere Buddha's unseeing eyes saw it all as he had seen it all before and he did it without moving his lips.

21. Our Lives in Their Hands

The day we had looked forward to with fearful anticipation finally arrived, our interview at the British Embassy. Today we would know, one way or the other, what our future held in store.

Whisky was really nervous. So was I, but doing my best not to show it.

As we walked to the Embassy we were getting the looks from every day Thai people that I now ignored, but looks that Whisky never, ever did get used to.

'They think I bar girl because walk with farang' she told me sadly in the early days of our relationship. The word 'farang' is used widely to refer to white skinned westerners.

When we had Kevin with us it was completely different, everyone used to smile at us. There was a vivid contrast in the two situations, with Kevin and without Kevin. At times it had got so bad for Whisky that she would ask me to walk behind her or in front of her.

But today we walked side by side the short distance to the British Embassy.

We arrived at the Embassy at the appointed time and sat, waiting to be called for interview, in the large reception area. We had handed in all the relevant documents that were required by the Embassy to help them make their decision, but this decision would be made mostly from the interview, of that much I was sure.

There were many other couples waiting in the same area. Looking at them, one could see the problem the Embassy officials had in judging who was genuine and who wasn't. There were couples who looked well matched but also really old looking men with very young looking Thai girls. Whisky pointed out the ones she thought were probably bar girls. They were mostly the ones with the older men.

Whisky's name was called for interview. My stomach turned over. She winked at me, showed me that she had her fingers crossed, walked over to the appointed door, and entered. I then had a wait of about forty five minutes before Whisky reappeared. She sat down beside me looking really flushed.

'Very difficult Mike. They ask many questions. Where we meet, where we go together, what we ....'

She was interrupted by the request for me to go for my interview. I squeezed her hand, told her not to worry but keep her fingers crossed. I then went through the dreaded door.

It was just as Clive had told me. There was a seat for me to sit on, which I did at the request of the Embassy official who sat behind a reinforced glass screen. There was a microphone facing me and I could see another on his side of the glass. As Clive had said, it all felt very cold and impersonal.

However the gentleman on the other side of the glass couldn't have been nicer. He asked five or six questions, very politely, about how Whisky and I met originally and where we had been together. He asked about Kevin and what we planned for him in the future. All logical questions that I was well prepared to answer.

He had noticed from the documentation that I was a musician. He asked me what bands I had been in. I told him the name of the best known one. He then asked where we used to play. I told him of a few venues, including a well known pub in Smethwick. We then chatted about this pub which he apparently knew very well, small world I thought. Then suddenly he said,

'Well Mr. Smith, we can certainly grant your fiancee a visa.'

'Really!?' I almost yelled at him.

'You sound surprised,' he replied.

'Yes, frankly I am. I have been dreading this day for ages, my life in your hands so to speak. Back in England I did a lot of research into the whole subject of settlement visas. I met many people that the British Embassy had failed to give a visa to and became very concerned. I even saw a lawyer in London who was going to charge me around five thousand pounds to prepare a case to present to you. He even suggested manipulation of the truth where he thought necessary. In the end we decided to come along with the truth and hope that it was good enough.'

'Mr Smith,' he said with a very kindly tone in his voice. 'We are not hard people to convince when presented with the truth, we just don't hear it that often. So all I would like to do now is wish you and your fiancee every happiness in the future.'

Well knock me down with a feather! We'd done it! 'YES!'

I thanked him for his kindness and returned to the seat next to Whisky to tell her the news. At first she wouldn't believe me. She thought I was pulling her leg. Eventually it sank in and she was elated.

'It's strange Mike, but Thai lady interpreter that interviewed me knows mother.'

'Your mother knows staff at the British Embassy?' I asked, utterly aghast.

'Yes, Mom works at sports centre where many farang go,' she replied.

'Why didn't you tell me this earlier?' I asked.

'Would it have helped?' she replied innocently.

'Oh I don't know, and it doesn't matter now anyway, we're on our way to England.'

'Not necessarily!' replied the Phantom Bangkok Bum Biter.

Our interview was on a Tuesday and we were due to fly to England on the following Sunday.

Back at Thai House everyone was happy for us and wishing us luck. Whisky went shopping for things she would need in England that she assured me could only be bought in Thailand.

Jim and I were sitting in our well used seats in the bar supping a beer and discussing birth signs, for some odd reason.

'What is Whisky's birth sign?' Jim asked.

'I don't know for sure, but I think her birthday is some time in February. I'll have a look at her passport,' I replied, and extracted it from the document folder I had on the floor beside me.

I opened it, looked at it, and looked at it again.

Oh good grief! How on earth had I missed this? I'd checked everything, so how had I missed this?

In Whisky's passport it said in the name section Mrs, not Miss but Mrs.

I told Jim and asked if he thought it was going to cause a problem.

'Oh dear,' he said. 'After everything you've been through. Of course it will cause a problem,' Jim looked very serious.

'In my opinion Mike, the British Embassy have made a big error here. They have granted a visa to allow a Thai lady to get married who, on paper, is already married.'

'That's what I thought Jim. What the hell do I do about this one?'

'Very tricky,' he said. 'Even if they don't pick it up at customs and you do get to England, no one is going to marry a married lady. You need some proof that she was never legally married.'

'That's more documents then, isn't it?' I asked

'It is, and you haven't much time. Can't see it being done by Friday. It's too late to even try today, so that leaves you with two days. I have a feeling that this is going to be complicated. I just don't know about the complexity of the situation. We'll need to speak to my wife. Tor is more knowledgeable about Thai law than I am, and if she doesn't know, she'll probably know a man who does.'

Jim called Tor over to where we were sitting, showed her the passport, and explained the situation.

'They'll need an official document stating that Whisky was never married before and that she only changed her name from Miss to Mrs to give respectability to her son. The passport office obviously produced this from the family document.' Tor said in response.

'We know that much,' said Jim. 'But how quickly can all this be done?'

'One day,' said Tor.

'No way!' said Jim

'One day,' repeated Tor more emphatically.

They then proceeded to have a row about it which ended up with Jim betting five hundred baht that it couldn't be achieved in a day. Tor accepted the bet and said that she would take Whisky and myself to the appropriate offices the following day.

'Be in reception at nine o'clock and we'll prove the silly farang to be wrong,' Tor said encouragingly.

Whisky returned from shopping looking very happy and eager to show me what she had bought. I did not want to spoil her fun, and so I waited for her to finish before I told her of the latest little inconvenience we had to face. She was not a happy lady. She felt it was her fault. It took a little time for me to convince her that it wasn't her fault.

'I should have spotted it, and so should the Embassy. So if it's anyone's fault it's mine,' I reassured her.

She eventually seemed quite happy to accept that it was my fault and we discussed what had to be done.

She would need to get some family documents, that the authorities would need to see, from her home before nine o'clock in the morning. This simple task was not that simple. She would have to wait till her father was asleep, creep into the house, get the papers, and creep out again. All a bit 'cloak and dagger' really.

We waited until about midnight and took a taxi to Whisky's home. This was to be the first time I had been anywhere near the place where she lived. I of course had to wait in the taxi some distance from the house while Whisky crept in to retrieve the papers we needed.

The journey from Thai House had made me realise something. Often on the phone from England I had heard Whisky say that she was very tired. I had often wondered if she should be taking some of the vitamin tablets that my mother always swore by, because for a young woman she always sounded tired. I suddenly realised why she got so tired. I knew her shift at the Huntsman was ten hours. Add to that two hours travelling to work and about one hour return, which makes thirteen hours. On top of all that add one hour each way walking the distance from the main highway to her home, and in that oppressive heat. I shook my head in disbelief. No wonder she was always tired, she did all that every day, six days a week, and then looked after her father and Kevin. I decided there and then that if we ever did get to England I would make sure that Whisky would do nothing for at least a month, except take a few vitamin pills that is.

She returned to the taxi about thirty minutes later with the papers we needed.

'Everything all right?' I asked.

'Yes,' she replied, sounding a little out of breath. 'Very exciting. Dad wake up and I had to hide till asleep again, very exciting, heart go bump bump.'

'I wish we didn't have to do it like this Whisky,' I said. 'I feel really sorry for your Dad. Are you sure we can't tell him what's going on?'

'No way, he be very angry. He lose much face in community if know I marry farang. Best he not know. One day we tell him, not now. Trust me Mike, I know what I do'

With that I had to be content. As Jim had said 'Leave it alone Mike, let them deal with it.' But I still felt sorry for the man. He was a father like myself. If I was him I think I would be more hurt by the deceit than by the fact that my daughter was doing something I didn't agree with, but then I don't hold such strict views on marriage between people of different faiths as he obviously did. 'Each to his own' as they say, but it was still very sad. We returned to Thai House and tried to get some sleep. Not an easy task when you're back in the land of insecurity and uncertainty.

At nine o'clock, on the dot as there was five hundred baht at stake, we all piled into Tor's car. We then started to drive up the Sukhumvit Road. When I say drive I'm being a little over enthusiastic. For the first hour the car's speedometer stayed very firmly below ten miles an hour. The traffic situation in Bangkok is well known world-wide, we were basically in a slow moving car park. But arrive at our destination we eventually did, to be told that we were in the wrong place, so back into the car again.

This was to be the pattern of the day. I just got hotter and hotter waiting for Tor and Whisky to go from one office to another getting all the relevant papers together. It all apparently had to be done in stages. Document A had to be got so that it could be shown to get Document B and so on. After much to-ing and fro-ing we finally arrived back at the area office we had started out at to get the final document. It was now only a matter of a bit of pen pushing and we were home and dry.

'Oh no your not,' said the Phantom Bangkok Bum Biter. 'You need the final document witnessed by two people, both Thai, and both must have known Whisky for at least five years.'

Tor said that she wasn't going to be done out of her five hundred baht so close to the finishing post, and walked off down the street. When she returned about fifteen minutes later she was with a Thai man who had apparently known Whisky for five years, knew that she was never legally married, and was prepared to sign the document stating that fact. He was also a Muslim.

Now wasn't that a coincidence! I had to give him a little thank you gift of course for being so conveniently in the right place at the right time. That's what I like about Bangkok, there's always someone you can find willing to help you out. Tor was the other witness for us.

While all the relevant papers were being signed and witnessed, which took some time, I decided to take a short stroll. I turned up a side street which turned out to end at a klong. There was a small temple on my left and I could hear voices from within the open windows. I could see there were Buddhist priests teaching children who sat on the floor before them. What mostly took my eye was a priest nursing a lap top computer as he sat crossed legged. The incongruity of the situation was intriguing. Here was modern technology hand in hand with a civilisation that went back for centuries. Just as the buildings worked side by side, the old and the new, I pondered on the wonders of civilisation forever changing, forever reshaping itself. I watched for a while the dancing reflections in the waters and wondered how the world would change for these youngsters in the temple and indeed for Kevin, my new son.

I retraced my steps back to the area office building to find Whisky and Tor waiting for me with all the papers we required duly signed and sealed. Tor was very happy that she could return to Thai House and ask Jim for the five hundred baht. All in all a successful trip. That evening, after Jim got over his depression, we all went out for a well deserved celebration meal.

21. House Buying, Thai Style

In my life to date I had been involved in the purchase of four houses in England. Each one took time to buy. Each one required a solicitor to draw up the necessary papers. Each one required a survey to be done. Every building society had to check many things before they would lend the money.

Not quite like that in Bangkok! It took approximately one hour to buy Whisky's Mom a house, not counting travelling time of course.

We had seen some leaflets about new houses being built on the airport side of Bangkok. They were small and quite western looking.

Four of us went to have a look. Grandma, Mom, Whisky and me.

It took nearly the whole of the morning to get there and most of the afternoon to get back. In the hour in between travelling we bought one of these small houses.

The journey to the building site was a good opportunity to see the chaos that is Bangkok. There doesn't seem to be any regulation to what you can build and where. The variety of buildings you pass travelling through this capital city is amazing. Skyscrapers stand cheek by jowl with tin roofed shacks. What this seeming lack of control creates however is a wealth of colourful variety not seen back home in England. Yet somehow the whole hodge-podge works. There is harmony in the contrast - rich and poor living side by side.

In all my trips to this city I have never seen any violence or ever felt threatened. Yet there is everything there that you would think would result in violent outbursts. The population of Bangkok seem to have a high level of tolerance to things that would frustrate and anger their western counterparts. The traffic situation is but one example of this tolerance. I never ever saw, what we call in the west, road rage although I did see many times good reason for it existing.

Eventually we arrived at the building site and were shown into a little office. We were then introduced to the site agent, an attractive Thai lady, very smartly dressed in a pink suit. I didn't understand most of what was being said and had to rely on Whisky to tell me.

'House not built yet.' Whisky told me. 'But will be like picture in leaflet.'

'Can you ask the agent if there is a similar house, that is finished, available to view?' I asked Whisky to ask the lady house agent.

Whisky did so and we were taken into another office and shown a model of what the house would look like.

'Whisky, I don't think you quite understand. I want to see a full size house that these people have built. Is that possible?'

More words spoken in Thai and then hoots of laughter.

'Follow lady,' said Whisky, still laughing.

We walked down a long road with houses on either side in various stages of completion, finally arriving at one that looked very nearly finished, and that bore some resemblance to the picture and the model back in the office.

The lady agent showed us around talking non stop as she did. I thumped a few walls, banged my foot on a few floors, and tested the flushing capabilities of the toilet. All in a vain attempt to indicate to the agent that I was a very discerning house purchaser. I don't think it had the desired effect but at least it gave me something to do while everyone was chatting away very seriously in Thai.

As far as I know, which isn't much 'cos I'm a musician, the house seemed fine, and Whisky's Mom was delighted with it. We returned to the office and papers were produced. There was a plan of the site with the various plots indicated. Whisky's Mom chose plot forty seven, and the agent wrote on the papers in front of us that were all in Thai.

Whisky then explained what we had to do. It was quite

complicated, so you'll have to concentrate.

'Mom signs paper, you pay deposit, we go Thai House.'

'You mean that's all we have to do. No survey, no solicitor, no area searches and nobody asking questions about if we can afford the mortgage?'

'That's it Mike,' Whisky replied.

'And this is all right with everybody?' I asked perplexed.

'Yes fine,' said Whisky.

'You are sure you know what we are doing?' I asked, still not believing how simple this all was compared to the west.

'Yes Mike, you worry too much, Chai Yen Yen, take it easy,' Whisky replied.

The papers were duly signed and we'd bought a house. One hour, start to finish.

Whisky's Mom kept insisting that it wasn't her house - it was ours. She would take care of it for us. She is a lovely lady, has worked extremely hard all her life and devoted herself to the needs of her children. She was now part of my family and it made me happy to be part of achieving this for her.

21. Glad all Over

Soon it would be time for us to be returning to England. Whisky had to make another trip home to collect her belongings. As she entered our room on her return she was carrying a small bag, about the size of a sports bag.

'Hi,' I said. ' Have you left your cases in reception?'

'No cases, just bag,' she replied.

'Is that all you're taking?' I asked, 'You are intending to stay aren't you?'

Whisky laughed. 'This all I have worth taking really.'

She was leaving her home country to live in England and all she had was an overnight bag. Amazing! So she really was telling the truth regarding her one and only dress.

'We go to shopping now,' I said firmly, having learnt to speak English Thai style, and having watched Whisky empty out the meagre contents of her bag.

'Don't argue, you need clothes and it's less expensive to buy them here than in England.'

'Fine,' she replied with no argument at all. 'You give me four thousand baht (about one hundred pounds.) I go to shopping with my sister. But I pay back in England from job.'

'Can't I go with you?' I asked feeling disappointed.

'No good, you know shop want more if see farang. Better me and Janjira,' she replied.

'So I'll get to meet your sister Janjira at last?' I asked.

'Yes, but she more beautiful than me, she more clever than me.'

Whisky looked quite perturbed.

'Is that why I haven't met her yet Whisky?'

I could see from her expression what was in her mind so I continued, 'Do you really think that even if she is more beautiful and more intelligent than you, which I doubt, it would make the slightest bit of difference to how I feel about you?'

'Don't know really, you are man,' Whisky said. 'My ex-husband always fancy her.'

Whisky had a pretty low opinion of men as a gender. I suppose having been brought up in Bangkok, surrounded by the high profile sex industry, influenced her opinion somewhat, plus the fact that Kevin's father had deserted them for another woman. Only time and better experiences would change that opinion.

When I did finally meet Janjira later that day I had to agree that she was very beautiful and intelligent but in my opinion no more so than Whisky. They were both extremely attractive ladies, in every sense of the word.

Bangkok has many parks, beautifully kept and the four of us went for a walk in one of them, Lupinee Park. Janjira spoke English very well. She chatted animatedly to me while Kevin played football with his Mom. I felt sure I was on trial. Only natural really. I felt that it was important to Whisky that Janjira liked me. Luckily we seemed to hit it off quite well. Later Whisky told me that Janjira had expressed the view that Whisky should go to England with me. Just as well really because I'd already bought the tickets!

The following day saw Whisky and her sister out shopping again. Bad news I thought to myself, they are really getting the hang of this shopping lark.

I spent the day doing a bit of shopping myself, the odd present or two for my children and others I needed to placate. I also popped back to the very first hotel I had stayed in many months ago to say goodbye to Jym and the rest of the very kind staff there. I then went and stood on one of the pedestrian bridges that cross the Sukhumvit Road. I looked up the road, turned round and looked down the road. I could see the Landmark Hotel, McDonalds, Thai House, and The Ambassador Hotel. I could see the road that led to the agency, and the road that led to the first hotel I had stayed in. I could even see the little man still trying to show people his photographs of ladies of the night. It occurred to me that the majority of my time in Bangkok had been spent in half a square mile of this vast city. I didn't know Bangkok well at all I thought but I do know well this half a square mile. Back in

England many times I would close my eyes and see it all again, vividly.

When I returned to Thai House, Jim told me that everyone was upstairs in my room. As I entered the room I could see Whisky, her Mom, Janjira, all shoving things into cases and Kevin pulling things out of cases. I looked at them all and smiled. I was so lucky.

'Are you sure we need all this rice?' I asked Whisky, 'We can buy rice in England you know?'

'Different to England rice,' Whisky replied.

'How do you know? You've never been to England.'

'I just know!' Whisky replied firmly. 'Good greeps Mike. You big pain in the bum. Go have drink with Jim, leave us to do. Better way of doing.'

As they were all now laughing at me I left them to it, still thinking we had far too much rice.

'Only the airport to worry about now then,' Jim said, matter of factly.

'Worry about! What do you mean worry about?' I asked, wondering what he knew that I didn't.

'Oh, no, nothing. You'll probably be all right,' he replied.

'Jim, stop pulling my plonker! What are you on about?'

'People have been known to be turned back at the airport you know. I just hope all the documents and Visas are all right. I still wonder about the one Tor got done for you.'

'You just want your five hundred baht back. All the papers are fine, as you well know. You're just trying to get me going you old fart!'

He laughed.

'Just don't forget the Phantom Bangkok Bum Biter. He's always lurking and waiting to pounce.'

'They can't buy air tickets can they?' I asked.

'Who?' Jim asked.

'Phantom Bangkok Bum Biters,' I replied.

We both laughed and ordered another beer.

A bit later that evening I walked alone over to The Huntsman Pub for one last look at the place that had so drastically changed my life. I had one beer and one coffee, listened to the band for a while, and left after saying goodbye to everybody. I'd loved that place, and at times I'd hated that place, but one thing was for sure, I would never forget The Huntsman Pub.

Back at the ranch, packing was completed and all we now had to do was wait for the taxi to take us to the airport. It duly arrived, cases were deposited in the boot, fond farewells were exchanged with Jim and Tor with promises to write, and we were on our way.

Believe it or not nothing happened on the way to the airport, no accidents, no punctures, nothing, we just arrived, very boring.

Same thing checking in, no problems, except for a charge for excess weight. I knew we had too much rice!

We all went up to the cafeteria on the first floor and stayed there chatting until it was time to board.

Whisky's Mom thanked me for the house and I thanked her for her wonderful daughter, and we both laughed. It had been decided that until the new house was finished Kevin would live at his great grandmother's home.

I don't think the little boy really understood what was going on. He was just excited to be in a big airport. When we all said our goodbyes he looked very serious. He now knew his mother was going somewhere and probably felt insecure. When Whisky and I finally walked away towards the passport control doors he just followed us. It was all very difficult really. He had to be held by his grandmother before we could go through into departure. This upset Whisky who had very bravely held back her tears in front of her son. Once we were finally in the departure lounge she sat down and sobbed.

I put my arm round her shoulders without saying anything, what could I say? She was going to the other side of the world without the little person who meant more to her than anyone. She eventually regained her composure, wiped her eyes, smiled at me, and said,

'Okay Mike, we go now.'

Buddha sighed with relief and winked.

About thirty minutes after take off the stewardess asked us what we would like to drink. I asked for my usual, a whisky.

'No Mike, not whisky, whisky no good for you, give you bad headaish.'

I looked at her and she suddenly realised what she had said. We both laughed.

'You glad all over Mike?' Whisky asked.

'I feel wonderful, never felt better,' I replied, thinking she was far too young to remember 'The Dave Clark Five'

'No, I mean you pleased no more Bangkok?' she said.

'Oh I see. Well I'm glad we're finally on our way to England but in many ways I'll miss Bangkok. We'll come back very soon Whisky, for Kevin. He's in good hands with your Mom and it won't be for too long.'

'I know,' she said, her thoughts trailing through the clouds and the jet stream, 'I miss him already.'

Her gaze went down to her home city passing far below us. The sunlight glinted and dazzled from a hundred rooftops of temples where The Buddha reposed in silent contemplation of the fate of all of us and I reflected that perhaps he shed a tear for his departing children.

When we arrived at Heathrow around ten o'clock that early July morning the weather was fairly overcast and although not cold, Whisky felt a distinct difference to Bangkok. It took ten minutes for me to go through passport control and I stood in England waiting for Whisky to wind her way round the barriers of no man's land crammed with queues of foreign visitors. Finally she was through and standing by my side. It felt wonderful. I thought of Clive and Karla and hoped that they one day would be standing where Whisky and I now stood.

As both Wilf and Keith had done the 'picking me up at the airport' bit, it was Phil who had the job this time. At least I was fair in sharing around favours. He had come down to Heathrow in my car, a red Toyota Celica. The journey back to The Midlands would be one of the last in my 'large red penis extension' as Wilf used to call it.

The 'piper' who has to be paid, was now playing tunes directly through my letter-box, so the car had to be sold quickly.

As we set off up the motorway the clouds parted and the sun came out. It didn't go back in for weeks. It was the beginning of summer 1995 and a glorious time for Whisky to start to get to know England, and for England to get to know Whisky.

The first thing to amaze her was that the traffic moved freely. The next was how wonderfully green everything was. I would, through the eyes of Whisky, see my country in a new light. All the things I had come to take for granted she made me look at again and thereby appreciate much more than before. With Whisky's unknowing help I became proud to be British once again.

23. Three Best Men

Everyday life with Whisky is never ever dull. There is always something to laugh about. She is so naturally funny. I asked her once if people in Thailand found her funny.

'No, not really, they all thought I crazy,' she replied.

She had only been in the country a few days and was feeling ill.

'What's the matter Whisky?' I asked her. 'You don't look at all well.'

'Do not know, very strange, noodle in, noodle out, nothing happen, stomach die.'

It isn't just the wonderful ways she phrases things that make her funny. It's her whole approach to life that is so refreshing.

She had always wanted to learn to ride a bike. In Thailand a bike would have been a luxury, so she never had the opportunity to learn. I held the saddle for her, round and round our back lawn, for about thirty minutes until she had achieved some degree of balance. I then came indoors to make a cup of tea. Suddenly I saw her on the road outside our house, attempting to ride off. I rushed out to stop her. Too late! She'd gone peddling off down the wrong side of the road. Thank goodness there were no cars coming. However there was a Mini parked on the one side. She wobbled a bit, I heard a high pitched scream, and then she smashed into the back of it. She picked herself and the bike up off the road, pushed it back along the pavement to where I was standing and said,

'Mike, you no tell me where brake are!' looking really disgusted.

She now rides a bike well, usually in her little duffel coat with the hood over her head, followed by all the young children of our street, in a line behind her. She looks just like ET. You know the bit in the film where the children are on their bikes following ET up into the sky? Well that's what I see daily, I'm married to ET!

It's not just the children who love Whisky, it's everyone she meets. She is a unique lady.

When my children first met her they just hugged her, quite naturally, without any shyness at all. From that first meeting Whisky has been a good friend to both of them, and they love her dearly. She never shouts at them, and never tells them off, she's more like a big sister to them both and has earned their trust and respect. In return my children took little Kevin into their hearts as a brother when he finally arrived in England.

The one problem that I do now have is when at times I have to chastise any of my three children Whisky puts her arm round their shoulders and just looks at me. It is impossible to tell them off with Whisky consoling them before I even start.

She has changed this house completely without moving one piece of furniture. She's utterly changed the atmosphere. Everyone is a lot more laid back and happier for it. Somewhere between England's 'You have to be there on time or else' and Thailand's 'Chai Yen Yen' there is a great way to live.

We have our disagreements from time to time of course, especially when she insists on putting chilli powder on my sacred baked beans.

To be serious though there have been times when the very different cultures have clashed.

On one occasion when we had one such clash she stormed out of the house with what seemed every intention of walking back to Thailand. I have heard it said that eastern women are considered subservient, especially to men. Well let me utterly dispel this delusion. There is, as I have sometimes discovered to my cost, nothing subservient about Whisky.

We are constantly learning from each other and about each other, like any other married couple.

Yes, we did finally get married properly, at Lichfield registry office. As I couldn't decide which of my three good friends to have as best man, I asked them all. It was decided between them however that Wilf would do the speech, being the natural cabaret artist that he is.

It was a lovely day. We were married at noon. British noon, not Thailand noon, so everyone was there on time. The reception was held in our back garden that same evening and we had about fifty guests. Good old Eric plus his video camera was with us all day and filmed the entire event, mainly so that we could send a copy to Whisky's Mom.

My wife looked gorgeous in the same long white evening gown she had worn at Thai House for our engagement party.

As dusk fell on that warm English summer night, Wilf, a little wobbly, as he'd been drinking all day, gave us all the benefit of his experience in public speaking. Below is the edited version, you'll be happy to know.

'Mike rang me last week, told me he was getting married and asked me to be best man. Having first made sure it wasn't going to affect me dole, I agreed. So as I've only had a couple or three days to prepare this speech, it won't be too deep and meaningful.'

'Or too long hopefully!' added Keith.

'Keith, do please be quiet, I'm trying to do the best for my pal 'ere, please don't heckle!'

'Sorry Wilf,' Keith replied.

'I've known Mike for twenty seven years, which is a long time to know anyone, especially Mike.'

Yelps of agreement from the assembled congregation!

'When he first told me about meeting Whisky I was very sceptical.'

'Surely not,' I said.

'Please don't interrupt me Mike, I really am doin' me best here pal!'

'Yes Wilf, sorry Wilf'

'It has to be said that I thought he was off his head and grasping at straws. Having now met Whisky I fully understand his determination and admire his staying power. I have only known Whisky for a few days but would like to say how much I am taken with her and how brave I think she is to have come to England, especially when she has had to leave her son in Thailand for the time being. But I'd just like to say to you Whisky that when you realise just what you've let yourself in for marrying Mike, don't come to me for the air fare back home, cos' I ain't got it!'

Hoots of laughter from the assembled congregation!

'Seriously though I wish you both every happiness in the future because it is obvious to me, and to anyone that bothers to look, that you are very much in love with each other. The fact that we are here to celebrate your marriage is credit to you both. So let's all raise our glasses to Mike and Whisky, Mr and Mrs Smith. Health and Happiness.'

Lots of cheers and applause from the assembled congregation!

Epilogue

At last we were married - properly married. The only sad part was the fact that my mother refused to attend. She was being her usual stubborn self, however the situation with my mother was eventually solved, by Whisky.

Family is very important in Thai culture and Whisky finally got fed up with what she saw as two stubborn people being stupid. She insisted I take her over to see my mother. I told her she would get absolutely nowhere doing this but she insisted. I dropped her off outside my mother's flat, accompanied by Emma and Kevin, and waited in the car for them to return. I knew for sure that I wouldn't have to wait long.

Wrong again!

I had to wait for about an hour. My wife's ability at drawing people to her still amazes me. Even my mother gave in to Whisky's charms, but insists on calling her Warune which she thinks is a beautiful, and far more respectable, name.

As I said in an earlier chapter Whisky and I returned to Bangkok, three months after our wedding in England, to get Kevin. The trip went very smoothly with no problems I'm happy to say. There was one incident that happened that was a little amusing. While Whisky and I were waiting in the British Embassy for them to issue Kevin's visa he piddled all over the waiting room floor. In my travels over the past year I had met many men who would have liked to shake Kevin's hand for this act of desecration, especially the guy with the sceptic tank.

However, as the British Embassy had been so kind to us on every occasion we had dealings with them, I got some tissue paper from the toilet and mopped up Kevin's little accident before anyone noticed.

Kevin has settled in well to his new life and is learning to speak English very quickly. My children love him very much.

He is a delightfully happy little boy. Down at the doctor's surgery they call him Soda!

Originally I went to Bangkok because I was lonely and desperately needed someone to share my life. In the end I was very, very lucky to find Whisky and Kevin, but I also found so much more. A new and better way of living, good friends, and a much greater understanding of myself.

Going to Thailand certainly changed my life and one day I think Whisky and I might well end up living there. I miss it very much, the chaos, the excitement, the beauty and the whole unique charm of the place.

But for the moment we are all living in England; Whisky, Emma, David, and Kevin, plus one dog, two cats, two chinchillas, one cockatiel with perfect pitch, and I've never been happier in my life.